Collins

Mental Maths

Ages 12–13

Concepts tested

Chapter Number	Chapters	Exercises
1.	Rational Numbers	1, 2, 5, 9
2.	Exponents	3, 5, 9
3.	Squares and Square Roots	6, 8, 9, 20
4.	Cubes and Cube Roots	5, 7, 8, 9, 20
5.	Playing with Numbers	4, 5, 9, 20
6.	Algebraic Expressions and Identities	10, 11, 14, 19
7.	Factorisation	11, 12, 14, 19, 20
8.	Linear Equations in One Variable	13, 14, 19, 20
9.	Percentage and Its Application	15, 16, 18, 19
10.	Compound Interest	17, 18, 19, 20
11.	Direct and Inverse Proportions	21, 22, 24, 30, 40
12.	Understanding Quadrilaterals	25, 29–34, 39, 40
13.	Practical Geometry	33, 34, 39, 40
14.	Area of Polygons	26, 29–34, 39, 40
15.	Visualising Solid Shapes	23, 24, 30, 40
16.	Mensuration of Three-dimensional Figures	26–30, 40
17.	Introduction to graphs	35, 38, 39, 40
18.	Data Handling	35, 36, 38, 39, 40
19.	Probability	37, 38, 39, 40

Introduction

About this book

- This book is part of *Collins Mental Maths*, a series to support the development of primary mathematical skills.
- The grid on page 2 shows which concepts are tested in this book.
- The 40 exercises provide a fun and instant way of testing understanding of these concepts on a weekly basis.
- The questions are presented in a variety of simple styles to make them accessible and engaging, even to more reluctant learners.
- The exercises become progressively more challenging, supporting steady advancement.
- Each exercise contains an element of revision, providing some questions of a similar level to the previous exercises.
- Solutions to all the questions in this book can be found on pages 45–48. They are presented in a format that matches the solution strips on the exercise pages, enabling easy checking. There is one mark available for each question.
- Special thanks to Ms Sumanjeet Kaur for providing content for this book.

Recording progress

- At the end of each exercise is a space for recording the number of correct solutions.

Score

- 'How well did I do?' on page 4 consists of a chart for recording the exercise marks. This not only helps to monitor progress, but also provides practice in handling data for a purpose and demonstrates the use of mathematics in an everyday situation. It also provides a simple visual record of exercise results.

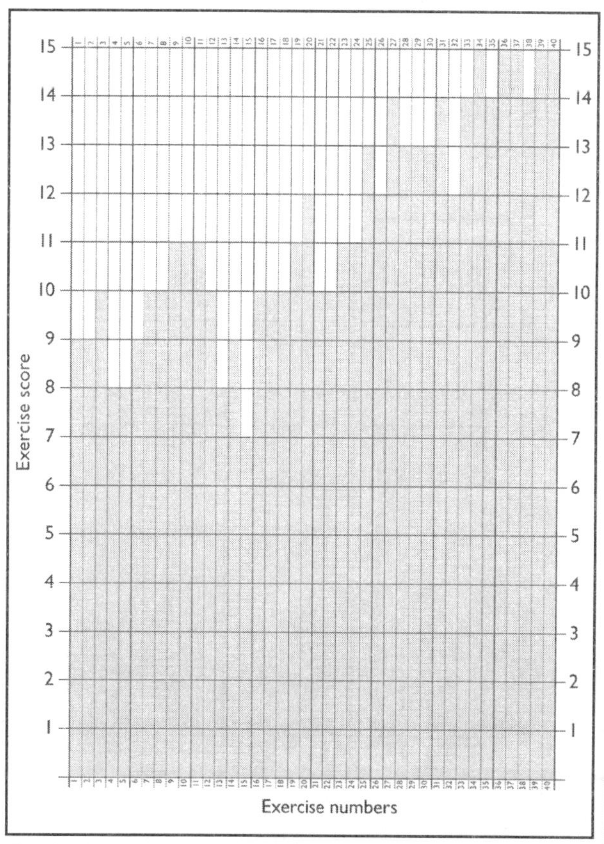

How well did I do?

Shade in your exercise scores on this chart.

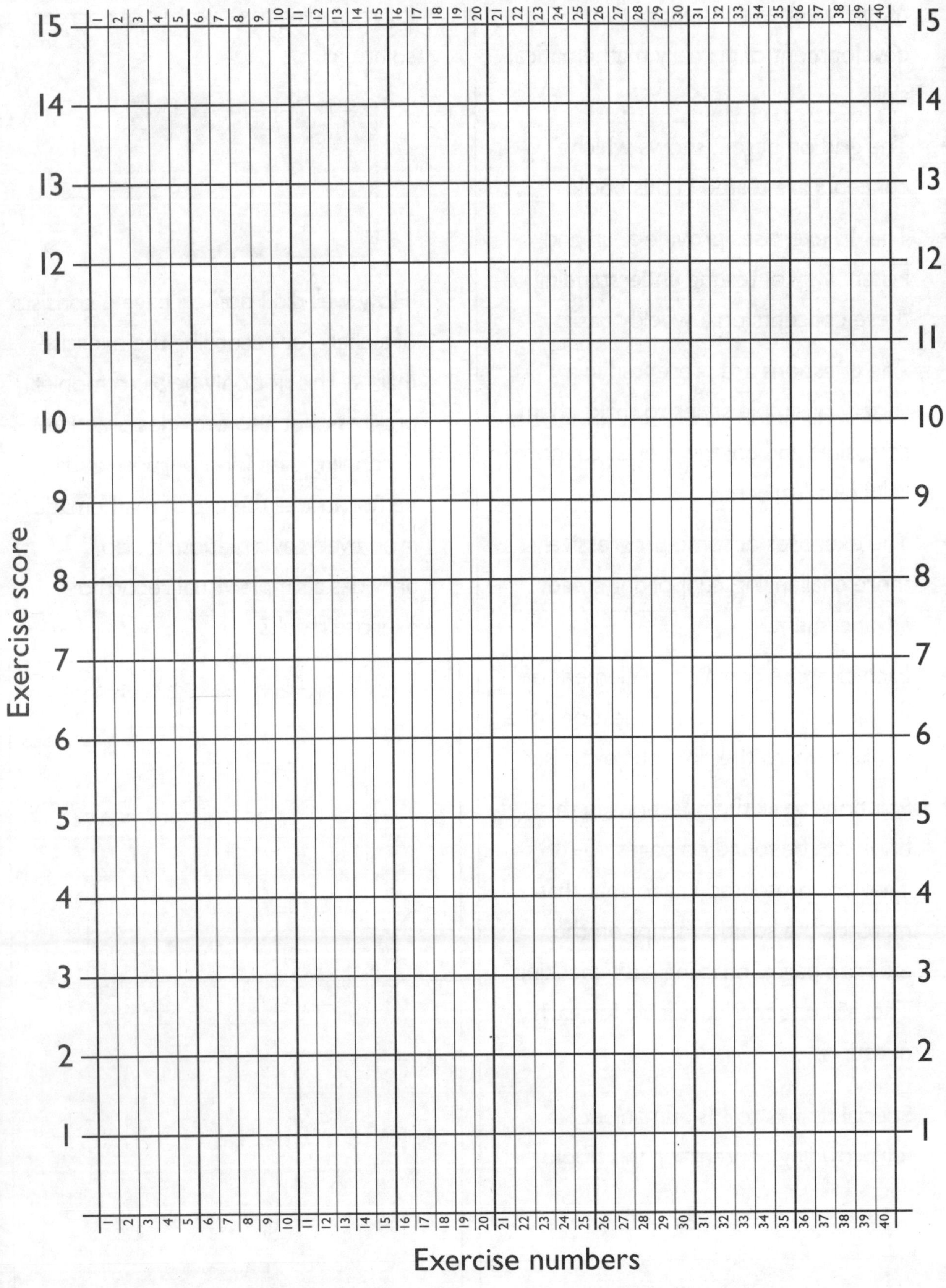

Exercise 1

1 Write the letter by which the $\frac{\text{Collection}}{\text{Set}}$ Of Rational Numbers is denoted. Give an example of a Rational Number.

2 Express $-\frac{6}{5}$ as a rational number with denominator -30.

3 Write a rational number with numerator $15 - 9$ and denominator $15 + 9$.

4 Express $\frac{21}{-49}$ in its standard form.

5 State which pair of rational numbers is equal.

(i) $\frac{7}{8}$ and $\frac{8}{7}$ (ii) $\frac{-3}{19}$ and $\frac{12}{-76}$.

6 Express zero as a rational number i.e. in the form of $\frac{p}{q}$.

7 Write the additive inverse of $\frac{17}{-90}$ and multiply it with multiplicative inverse of $\frac{7}{9}$.

8 Which two rational numbers are their own reciprocals?

9 If $\frac{p}{q}$ be any rational number and 'n' be any integer, then

$$\frac{p}{q} = \frac{p \times n}{q \times n}.$$

For what value of n will the statement be not valid?

10 Insert the missing number.

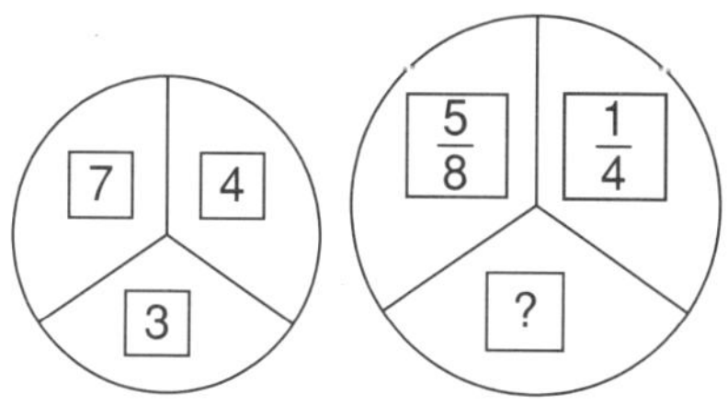

11 Write the product of $\left(-\frac{17}{36}\right) \times 0 \times \frac{52}{65} \times 10$.

12 Write the reciprocal of 'z', if $z \neq 0$.

13 If $\frac{1}{a} - \frac{1}{b} = \frac{1}{c}$, find the value of c.

14 A glass full of milk weighs $\frac{3}{4}$ kg and half full weighs $\frac{1}{2}$ kg. What is the weight of the glass ?

15 Calculate : $1 + \cfrac{1}{1 + \cfrac{1}{1 + \cfrac{1}{4}}}$.

Solutions

1
2
3
4
5
6
7
8
9
10
11
12
13
14
15

Score

Exercise 2

1. State the property used in $-\frac{1}{4}+\left[\frac{5}{7}+\frac{8}{12}\right]=\left[-\frac{1}{4}+\frac{5}{7}\right]+\frac{8}{12}$.

2. The sum of two numbers is -4. If one of them is $-\frac{12}{5}$, find the other number.

3. Find $(x+y)\div(x-y)$ if $x=\frac{5}{4}$ and $y=-\frac{1}{3}$.

4. Solve using appropriate property of Rational Numbers: $\frac{2}{5}\times\frac{1}{6}-\frac{1}{2}+\frac{2}{5}\times\frac{2}{3}$.

5. Write the reciprocal of $-\frac{7}{9}\times\frac{8}{15}$.

6. Write the smallest rational number that can be formed by using 2 of the given numbers, in the form of $\frac{p}{q}$
434, – 769, 933, – 203, 175, 355.

7. Find the value of '*n*' so that the numbers are ordered from greatest to least.
$\frac{11}{12}, \frac{n}{4}, \frac{2}{3}$.

8. Write any two rational numbers between $-\frac{1}{4}$ and $\frac{1}{4}$.

9. If $-\frac{2}{7}, -\frac{5}{7}$ and $-\frac{1}{7}$ are to be represented on a number line, which distance would you divide into 7 equal parts; from 0 to 1 or from 0 to – 1 ?

10. Write a rational number that cannot be represented on a number line.

11. What number should be subtracted from $\frac{7}{9}$ to get $\frac{2}{3}$?

12. $-1\times\left[-\frac{2}{3}\times\frac{3}{5}\right]$
$=[\text{..........}\times\text{..........}]\times\frac{3}{5}$.

13. The product of two rational numbers is – 17. If one of the numbers is 12, find the other.

14. In a school of 5044 students, ratio of girls to ratio of boys is 5:8. $\frac{1}{5}$th of the girls and $\frac{1}{8}$th of the boys took part in a school camp. Write the fraction of the total strength that took part in the camp.

15. If $\frac{a}{b}$ and $\frac{c}{d}$ are any two rational numbers then $\frac{a}{b}\div\frac{c}{d}=\frac{a}{b}\times$..........

Solutions

1
2
3
4
5
6
7
8
9
10
11
12
13
14
15

Score

Exercise 3

1. Compute the sixth power of – 3.

2. Write q^6 in the expanded form.

3. Find the value of $\left(-\frac{3}{4}\right)^2 \times \left(-\frac{2}{5}\right)^3$.

4. Let $\frac{a}{b}$ be any rational number and 'n' be any integer.
   Then $\left(\frac{a}{b}\right)^{-n}$ is defined as

   $\left(\frac{a}{b}\right)^{-n} = \left(\frac{b}{a}\right)$................

5. Evaluate $\left(\frac{208}{109}\right)^0$.

6. Find the value of $\left(-\frac{3}{4}\right)^{-2}$.

7. Evaluate $\left(-\frac{2}{5}\right)^7 \div \left(-\frac{2}{5}\right)^5$.

8. For a non zero rational number 'a', $(a^3)^{-2}$ is equal to ....

9. $\left[-\frac{3}{2}\right]^{-1}$ = ...

10. Calculate: $\left(\frac{2}{3}\right)^5 \times \left(\frac{5}{7}\right)^5$

11. Find 'x' such that $\left(\frac{7}{5}\right)^{-5} \times \left(\frac{7}{5}\right)^{-11} = \left(\frac{7}{5}\right)^{8x}$.

12. By what number should $(-12)^{-1}$ be divided so that the quotient is $\left(\frac{2}{3}\right)^{-1}$.

13. When simplified, $(x^{-1} + y^{-1})$ is equal to ....

14. The value of $[2 - 3(2 - 3)^{-1}]^{-1}$ is ....

15. Radha received a chain letter. It was actually a prayer for world peace. She was asked to send its copies to 5 of her friends and instruct them to do the same. Find number of dispatched letters in the 5th round.

Solutions

1.

2.

3.

4.

5.

6.

7.

8.

9.

10.

11.

12.

13.

14.

15.

Score

Exercise 4

1. Write the general form of 7018.

2. Take any 2-digit number. Reverse its digits. Add the two numbers. Identify the number by which the sum is divisible, using the divisibility rules.

3. A number consists of 2-digits whose sum is 9. If 9 is subtracted from the number, the digits interchange their places. Find the number.

4. If 31z5 is a multiple of 3 as well as 9, what are the possible values of 'z'?

5. If the division N ÷ 5 leaves a remainder 4, which digits can occur at the one's place of 'N'?

6. Find Q in the addition

$$\begin{array}{r} 31Q \\ +\ 1Q3 \\ \hline 501 \\ \hline \end{array}$$

7. Find the values of A, B and C if

$$\begin{array}{r} AB \\ \times\ 3 \\ \hline C\,AB \\ \hline \end{array}$$

8. Check the divisibility of 6125 by 3.

9. In a digital display, which digit can display all ten digits from 0 to 9?

10. If the number 7715A8 is divisible by 4, which all digits can be put in the place of A?

11. Using the digits 1,3,4 and 0 only once (for each number), write four 4 –digit numbers which are exactly divisible by 5.

12. Continue this sequence: 1, 3, 6, 10, ..., ..., ... ,.......

13. Write the smallest value of x so that the number $4x032$ is divisible by 11.

14. Write a 3-digit number abc as $100a + 10b + c$. What is the condition on a, b and c such that this number is divisible by 11.

15. In a 2-digit number, the digit in the unit's place is four times the digit in the ten's place and the sum of the digits is 10. What is the number?

Solutions

1	
2	
3	
4	
5	
6	
7	
8	
9	
10	
11	
12	
13	
14	
15	

Score

Exercise 5

1. If 15a is divisible by 9, find the value of 'a'.

2. Simplify and write the answer $[4^{-1} \div 7^{-1}] \div [3^{-1} \div 7^{-1}]^{-1}$.

3. Is $-\frac{4}{17}$ the multiplicative inverse of $-4\frac{1}{4}$? Why or why not?

4. Write the number 745 in the form of $10a + b$.

5. If $x = \left[\frac{7}{3}\right]^{5} \div \left[\frac{7}{3}\right]^{3}$, find x^2.

6. State the property used in $-\frac{2}{9}\left[\frac{3}{5}-\frac{2}{9}\right] = -\frac{2}{9} \times \frac{3}{5} - \left[-\frac{2}{9}\right] \times \frac{2}{9}$.

7. Find a number whose cube is equal to the number itself but its square is not equal to the number itself.

8. Expand 18964.63 using exponents.

9. The thickness of a sheet of paper is 1.5×10^{-3} cm and the thickness of a human hair is 6×10^{-3} cm. Compare the two.

10. Find A, B C in addition

$$\begin{array}{r} 4C \\ +\ 98 \\ \hline AB3 \end{array}$$

11. Find the value of Q in the following multiplication.

$$\begin{array}{r} 1Q \\ \times\ Q \\ \hline 9Q \end{array}$$

12. Evaluate $4^{-\frac{1}{2}} \times 2^{\frac{1}{2}} \times \frac{2}{(8 \times 8^{-\frac{1}{2}})}$.

13. If $\frac{x}{y} = \left(\frac{2}{3}\right)^{-2} \times \left(\frac{3}{5}\right)^{-2}$, find $\left(\frac{x}{y}\right)^{-1}$.

14. Reciprocal of $\frac{-1}{y}$, where $y \neq 0$ is ....

15. Write the standard form of 4786.3460.

Solutions

1.
2.
3.
4.
5.
6.
7.
8.
9.
10.
11.
12.
13.
14.
15.

Score

Exercise 6

1. Write the number of non perfect square numbers between the squares of the numbers 'n' and '$n + 1$'.

2. What will be the digit at the units place in the square of 2157?

3. Write the number of consecutive odd numbers that should be added to get n^2.

4. Without adding find the sum of: $(1 + 3 + 5 + 7 + 9 + 11)$.

5. Express 121 as the sum of 11 natural numbers.

6. Write a Pythagorean triplet, whose one number is 16.

7. If $\sqrt{3+\sqrt{x}} = 5$, then find the value of x.

8. In a perfect square number containing 24 digits, what will be the number of digits in its square root?

9. Add a number 'x' with another number, which is, 11 times the first number and then take the square of the sum. What will be the result ?

10. Find the value $\sqrt{36}+\sqrt{49}$.

11. What is the smallest fraction that must be added to the square root of $5\frac{29}{100}$ so that the resulting number is a whole number?

12. What should come in the place of both 'x' in the following equation: $\left[\frac{x}{\sqrt{128}} = \frac{\sqrt{162}}{x}\right]$

13. $\sqrt{1.5625}$ = ...

14. If $3\sqrt{5} + \sqrt{125} = 17.88$, then what will be the value of $\sqrt{80} + 6\sqrt{5}$?

15. How many 2-digit numbers have 8 at the units place in their squares?

Solutions

1	
2	
3	
4	
5	
6	
7	
8	
9	
10	
11	
12	
13	
14	
15	

Score

Exercise 7

1. A number 'n' is called a perfect cube if in its prime factorization each factor appears .... times.

2. The number that can be expressed as the sum of two cubes in 2 different ways are called Hardy - Ramanujan Numbers. One of them is 1729. One combination is given here. Find the other.
$1729 = 12^3 + 1^3 = 1728 + 1$.
$1729 = \_\_ + \_\_ = \_\_ + \_\_$.

3. If a and b are any 2 natural numbers, then
$\sqrt[3]{\frac{a}{b}} =$ ....

4. Cube of an odd number is an .... number.

5. For any integer 'm', $m^2 < m^3$ may not be true. Give two such examples in which this statement does not hold true.

6. Write the digits whose cubes ends with them at the units place.

7. If you have a container in the shape of a cube that has a volume of 1331 m^3, then what is the area of each of the faces of this container?

8. Take a number 'x' and multiply it by 2. Take the cube of the resulting number. What is the ratio of this number to the cube of the resulting number?

9. Is the statement $\sqrt[3]{12^3 + 1^3} = \sqrt[3]{12^3} + \sqrt[3]{1^3}$ true?

10. The cube root of $2^3 \times 2^3 \times 2^3 \times 7^3 =$ ....

11. Sum of the cubes of the first 'n' natural numbers is equal to the square of their sum. Considering this statement, fill in the blanks:
$(1 + 2 + 3 + 4 + 5)^2 = (\ldots\ldots)^3 + (\ldots\ldots)^3 + (\ldots\ldots)^3 + (\ldots\ldots)^3 + (\ldots\ldots)^3$

12. Write the smallest number by which 192 should be divided to obtain a perfect cube.

13. $3^3+3^3+3^3=$ ....

14. Find the value of $125\sqrt[3]{a^6} - \sqrt[3]{125a^6}$.

15. $(504 + p)$ is a perfect cube number, whose cube root is p. Find the value of p.

Solutions

1	
2	
3	
4	
5	
6	
7	
8	
9	
10	
11	
12	
13	
14	
15	

Score

Exercise 8

1. Without adding, find the sum of : $1 + 3 + 5 + 7 + 9 + 11 + 13 + 15 + 17$.

2. Using the property of squares, find the value of $105^2 - 104^2$.

3. PQRS is a rhombus with in which PR = 12 cm and QS = 16 cm. Find the side length of this rhombus.

4. The area of a square field is $8464 m^2$. A man takes 3 rounds of the field. Find the distance covered by him.

5. Is 20,24,29 a Pythagorean Triplet?

6. Find the greatest 3-digit number that is a perfect square.

7. There are 500 children in a school for a P.Ed drill. They have to stand in such a manner that the number of rows is equal to the number of columns. How many children would be left out in this arrangement?

8. Find the smallest number by which 1250 must be multiplied to make it a perfect square. Also find the square root of the number so obtained.

9. Encircle the perfect cubes among the following. 27, 64, 125, 98, 100, –8000, 9000

10. A cubical piece of metal of dimensions 2 cm × 3 cm × 4 cm is melted. Some more of the metal is added and it is made into a cube. The cube has integral measures for its sides. What is the minimum amount of metal that is added and what is the size of the cube formed?

11. To collect rain water, Sajida made a cubical tank which can hold $91125 m^3$ of water. She uses this water for watering the plants of her garden. What is the height of this tank?

12. What would be the one's digit of the cube of 1024?

13. Cubes of the numbers ending with 2 and 8, are the numbers ending with .... and .... respectively.

14. Find the smallest number by which 675 must be multiplied to obtain a perfect cube.

15. The value of $45^2 - 65^2 + 20^2$ is ....

Solutions

1.
2.
3.
4.
5.
6.
7.
8.
9.
10.
11.
12.
13.
14.
15.

Score

Exercise 9

1. Compare $-\frac{17}{36}$ and $-\frac{18}{63}$.

2. Simplify $\left(-\frac{12}{7}\times\frac{35}{16}\right)\left(\frac{9}{5}\times\frac{4}{3}\right)$.

3. Find out three rational numbers between –5 and –6.

4. The simplified form of $425^{-\frac{4}{3}}$ is ....

5. The value of $x^{a-b}\times x^{b-c}\times x^{c-a}$ is ....

6. The area of a square is given by $A = s^2$. What will be the total area of 5 such similar squares, if the side of a square is 8 ft?

7. Find the square of 210 by using an appropriate property.

8. Using prime factorization, find the square root of 63504.

9. A welfare association collected ₹2,02,500 as donation from the residents. If each paid as many rupees as there were residents, find the number of residents.

10. Three numbers are in the ratio 2:3:4 and the sum of their cubes is 33957. Find the 3 numbers.

11. Express 6^3 as the sum of odd numbers.

12. The sides of a cube are doubled. Find the ratio between the volume of the first cube and the new cube.

13. If 43*x* 0 is a multiple of 2, where '*x*' is a digit, what might be the values of ''?

14. If a number is divisible by 9 and 17, by what other number will it be always divisible?

15. Find A, B, C and D in the following Cryptarithm:

$$\begin{array}{r} A\,B\,C \\ \times\quad 2 \\ \hline D\,A\,B \\ \hline \end{array}$$

Solutions

1.

2.

3.

4.

5.

6.

7.

8.

9.

10.

11.

12.

13.

14.

15.

Score

Exercise 10

1. Sanjay is 3 years older than Suchita. If Suchita's age is 'p' years, what is Sanjay's age?

2. Your age is 12 years now. What was your age 't' years ago? What will be your age 's' years from now?

3. Find the product of $7ab^2$, $-4a^2b$ and $-5abc$.

4. $8a^2 + ($ .... $) = -12a^2$.

5. $(3x^2 - 6x - 4) - (5 + x - 2x^2) =$ ....

6. Write the sum of $8x^2 - 5xy + 3y^2$, $2xy - 6y^2 + 3x^2$ and $y^2 + xy - 6x^2$.

7. What should be added to $8p^2 + 4 + 12p$ to make it a perfect square?

8. Simplify: $-7p[6q^2s] + 4q^2s[9p]$

9. $(5a^2 - 9) \times (-2a^2) =$ ....

10. $(x + 3)(x - 5) =$ ....

11. $(4a^3b^2 + 16a^2b + 8ab^2) \div 4ab =$ ....

12. $9m^2n^2 \times \frac{2}{3}mn \times -\frac{3}{4}m^3n^3 =$ ....

13. Divide $57s^3tu^2$ by $-19stu$.

14. Find the value of $x + x(x^x)$ when $x = 2$.

15. Find the value of $a^2 + 2(b^2 + c^2)$ if $a = 2$, $b = 1$ and $c = 3$.

Solutions

1.
2.
3.
4.
5.
6.
7.
8.
9.
10.
11.
12.
13.
14.
15.

Score

Exercise 11

1. Using suitable identity, find the product of $(2a + 4)(2a - 7)$.

2. Evaluate: $(104)^2$

3. Factorise $x^2 - x + y - xy$.

4. Factorise $m^4 - 256$.

5. Factorise using suitable identity: $q^2 - 10q + 25$

6. Factorise using suitable identity: $9x^2y^2 - 30xyz + 25z^2$

7. Divide $2x^2 - x - 3$ by $(x + 1)$ and write the quotient.

8. Write the value of 'x' if, $17x = 128^2 - 72^2$.

9. Evaluate: $(7.8 \times 7.8 - 2.13 \times 2.13)$

10. Factors of $3y^2 - 3y - 36$ are ....

11. $103 \times 97 =$ ....

12. Simplify: $[q^2 - 1][q^2 + 1][q^4 + 1]$

13. Obtain the volume of a rectangular box with length $= 7a^3$ units breadth $= 3a^2$ units and height $= 5a$ units.

14. If $\frac{a+1}{a} = 3$, find the value of $a^2 + \left(\frac{1}{a}\right)^2$.

15. If $ab = 8$ and $a + b = 6$, then find the value of $[a^2 + b^2]$.

Solutions

1	
2	
3	
4	
5	
6	
7	
8	
9	
10	
11	
12	
13	
14	
15	

Score

Exercise 12

1. Find the greatest common factor of $-4a^2b^2$, $12a^3b^3c$, $16a^5bc$.

2. Is $3(x-4) = 3x - 4$?

3. Factorize: $x^3 + 2x^2 - x$

4. Factorize: $2x^2 - 3ax + 1a^2$

5. Factorize: $(l + m)^2 - 4l\,m$

6. Factorize: $m^2 - 4\,mn + 4\,m^2$

7. Factorize by regrouping : $ab(x^2 + y^2) - xy(a^2 + b^2)$

8. Find the error and correct it: $\dfrac{4x}{4x+2} = \dfrac{1}{2}$.

9. Divide: $(m^2 + 21\,m - 46)$ by $(m - 2)$

10. Divide: $(2x^2 + 11x + 5)$ by $(2x + 1)$

11. Find and correct the error in the following.
$(a-7)(a-3) = a^2 - 21$.

12. Factors of $xy^2 + y(x-1) - 1$ are ....

13. Factorise : $\dfrac{1}{(x-y)^2} - 25z^2$

14. Divide the following after factorizing.

$$\frac{4-x^2}{(2-x)}$$

15. Factorise the following after re–grouping.
$x^3 + x^4 + x^5 + x^6$

Solutions

1.

2.

3.

4.

5.

6.

7.

8.

9.

10.

11.

12.

13.

14.

15.

Score

Exercise 13

1 An equation involving only .... polynomial is called a linear equation.

2 Find the value of x in: $2x - 3 = 5$

3 Find 'y' if $2y + 5(y - 2) = 4$

4 The dimensions of a rectangular field are $(3x + 1)$ and $(x + 7)$ units respectively. Find the area of the rectangle.

5 The difference of 11 and three times a natural number is 4. Find the number.

6 Twice a positive number is less than 30 by 4. The number is ....

7 Solve: $2(x - 3) + (2x - 5) = 5$

8 Find 'x' in the following figure

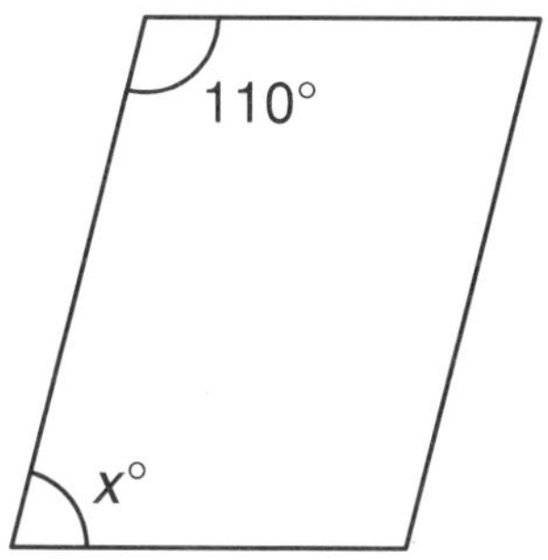

9 One–third of which number must be subtracted from $\frac{7}{11}$ to give $\frac{24}{55}$?

10 If $m = \frac{cab}{a - b}$, find the value of 'b'.

11 Solve for x: $2\left[x + \frac{1}{3}\right] - 4 = 0$

12 Two numbers are such that the ratio between them is 5:9. If 1 is added to the first number and 7 is added to the other, the ratio becomes 1:2. Find the numbers.

13 Find x in $\frac{(2x+3)-(x-5)}{(6x-1)-(4x+1)} = \frac{2}{3}$

14 The method used to simplify for 'x' in $\frac{ax+b}{cx+d} = \frac{m}{n}$ is ....

15

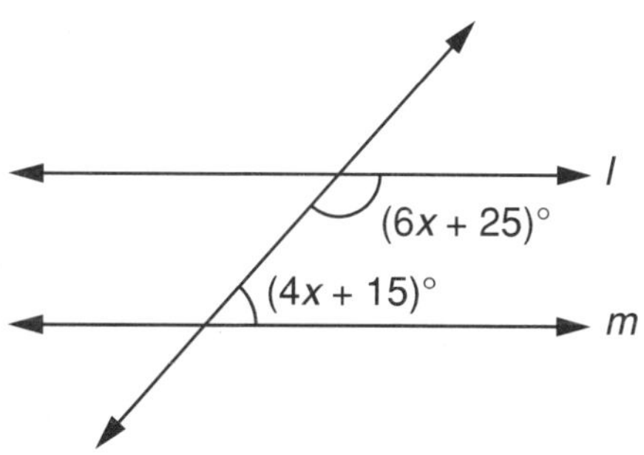

If l is parallel to m, find the value of x.

Solutions

1

2

3

4

5

6

7

8

9

10

11

12

13

14

15

Score

Exercise 14

1. Find the product : $(x + 3)(x^2 - 3x + y)$
2. Simplify : $(4x + 3y)^2 + (3x + 4y)^2$
3. Evaluate using appropriate identity: $(52)^2 - (48)^2$
4. Subtract $(4m + 6n)^2$ from $(4m - 6n)^2$.
5. Simplify $(x + y + z)(x + y - z)$.
6. Factorize: $x^4 - (x - y)^4$
7. Factorize: $y^2 + y - 56$
8. Factorize: $a^3 + a^2(x - y) - a(y + z) - z$
9. Factorize: $a^4b^4 - 81c^4$
10. Factorize: $2x^2 + 5x + 3$
11. The numerator of a fraction is 3 less than its denominator. If the numerator is increased by 1 and denominator is increased by 3, the fraction becomes equal to $\frac{1}{2}$. Find the original fraction.
12. Anil is 9 years older than Ajith. In 10 years, Anil will be twice as old as Ajith was 10 years ago. Find their present ages.
13. The length of a rectangle is 6 units more than its breadth. Its perimeter is 20 units. Find its length and breadth.
14. Solve : $y + \frac{3}{2} = y - \frac{4}{3}$
15. Solve : $\frac{x+b}{a-b} = \frac{x-b}{a+b}$

Solutions

1.
2.
3.
4.
5.
6.
7.
8.
9.
10.
11.
12.
13.
14.
15.

Score

Exercise 15

1. Convert 13% as a decimal.

2. Convert 5 : 20 into percentage.

3. Find x and y in $\frac{4}{5} = \frac{x}{100} = y\%$

4. Express 75mm : 15m as a per cent.

5. Convert $8\frac{1}{3}\%$ to a fraction.

6. Write the formula for S.P. when gain% is given.

7. The ratio of males and females in the population of a town is m : n. The percentage of females in the population is ....

8. x is 25%y. The percentage of y to x is

9. At a clearance sale, all goods are on sale at 45% discount. If I buy a skirt marked ₹600, how much would I pay for it?

10. After allowing a discount of 12% on the marked price of an article, it is sold at ₹880. Find its marked price.

11. Find discount in per cent when M.P. = ₹550 and S.P. = ₹425.

12. Using the terms Cost price, Marked price and Discount, write an inequality such that the sale results into a loss.

13. Given $x < y$, the percentage by which $x < y$ is ....

14. If the rate of VAT increases by 2%, then selling price of an article goes up by ₹140. Find the M.P. of the article.

15. Madhu bought a pair of bangles for ₹700. The sales tax charged is 5%. Find the bill amount and sales tax.

Solutions

1.

2.

3.

4.

5.

6.

7.

8.

9.

10.

11.

12.

13.

14.

15.

Score

Exercise 16

1. A boy spent 40% of his pocket money and is left with ₹54. How much money does he get as poket money?

2. Find the C.P if S.P = ₹470 and does 6% loss.

3. When C.P = ₹2012
Overhead Expenses = ₹500,
then final C.P = ...

4. When M.P = ₹1125,
Net Price = ₹1020, then
Discount = ...

5. Ashish sold a bicycle for ₹1080, at a profit of 20%. Find the C.P of the bicycle.

6. A chair was sold for ₹205 at a loss of 18%.
If the S.P had been ₹270, what would have been the gain or loss per cent?

7. Sea-Water contains 2.6% common salt. Find the weight of common salt in 2kg of sea-water.

8. If the C.P of 10 articles equals the S.P of 8 articles, find the profit or the loss per cent.

9. $S.P = M.P\left[\frac{100 - \text{Discount\%}}{100}\right]$
After allowing a discount of 20% on the marked price of lamp, a trader loses 10%. By what percentage is the marked price above the C.P?

10. What price should Aslam mark on a pair of shoes which costs him ₹1200 so as to gain 12%?

11. What single discount is equivalent to successive discounts of 30% and 20%?

12. By selling an article for ₹144, a man loses 10%. To gain 10%, he should sell it at the price ....

13. Anju buys old books from her friend for ₹550. She spends ₹50 for binding them. She then sells them off to another friend for ₹670. Find the gain or loss per cent.

14. An increase of 10% followed by a 10% decrease is same as ....

15. The cost of pair of roller skates at a shop was ₹450. The sales tax charged was 5%. Find the bill amount.

Solutions

1

2

3

4

5

6

7

8

9

10

11

12

13

14

15

Score

Exercise 17

1. Sarita invests ₹96,000 at 8% per annum simple interest. How much money will he get at the end of the year?

2. Raja borrowed ₹5000. At the end of 5 years, Raja had to pay back ₹6225. What was the rate of interest?

3. What principal will earn an interest of ₹576 at 6% per annum in 3 years?

4. In what time will the money deposited in a bank double itself if rate of interest is $12\frac{1}{2}$% p.a ?

5. Find the difference between simple interest and compound interest on ₹12,500 for 3 years at 12%p.a. compounded annually.

6. Find the compound interest on ₹15,000 for $1\frac{1}{2}$ years @ 8% p.a. if the interest is being compounded semi-annually.

7. Find the time taken for ₹12,500 to earn an interest of ₹1020@ 4% p.a. compounded annually.

8. Find principal if A = ₹79, 507, Rate = 15%p.a. compounded half yearly for 1.5 years.

9. Kritika borrowed ₹12,500 to purchase a refrigerator. What amount will she pay, if she uses the money for 146 days, the rate of interest being 18% per annum.

10. A sum of money placed at compound interest doubles itself in 4 years. It will amount to 8 times in ....

11. Depreciation = P[..............................]$^{----}$.

12. When interest is compounded quarterly A = ...

13. Which principal fetches more interest, the one compounded annually or half yearly or quarterly?

14. The value of an article depreciates by 10% annually. If the present value of the article is ₹1 Lakh, what will be its value after 2 years?

15. The population of the town was 1,60,000 , three years back. If it increased by 3%, 2.5% and 5% respectively in the last three years, find the present population.

Solutions

1.

2.

3.

4.

5.

6.

7.

8.

9.

10.

11.

12.

13.

14.

15.

Score

Exercise 18

1. What sales tax @ 5%, must you pay on the purchase of a computer hard drive that costs ₹15,500?

2. Rajat scored 20 out of 25 marks in English, 30 out of 40 in Science and 68 out of 80 marks in Mathematics. In which subject did he score the best percentage?

3. A table with a M.P ₹2400 was sold to a customer for ₹2200. Find the rate of discount allowed on the table?

4. A dealer purchased 250 bulbs for ₹10 each. However 12 bulbs got fused. She sold the remaining bulbs for ₹12 each. Find the gain or loss per cent in the transaction.

5. What price should Jamil mark on a pair of shoes which costs him ₹1200 so as to gain 12% after allowing a discount of 16%.

6. Due to 5% discount offered by a shop, price of T.V reduces by ₹3500. Find the discounted price of the T.V.

7. Price of a mobile phone including 10% VAT is ₹6600. Find the price of the mobile before VAT was added.

8. Your 3 years investment of ₹20,000 received 5.2% interest compounded semi-annually. What is the total return?

9. In how many years a sum of ₹6400 compounded quarterly @ 5% p.a will amount to ₹6561?

10. At what rate per cent per annum will a sum of ₹4000 yield compound interest of ₹400 in 2 years?

11. When interest is compounded quarterly, the rate gets divided by ....

12. The present value of a scooter is ₹38,640. Its value depreciated @ 8% per annum. What was the value of the scooter a year ago?

Solutions

Solutions
1
2
3
4
5
6
7
8
9
10
11
12

Score

Exercise 19

1. Population of 'J' block of a colony is 1000, in the beginning of January 2013. It increases @ 5%, every 6 months. Find the population of 'J' block colony after $1\frac{1}{2}$ years.

2. The marked price on an article in 2 different stores is the same.The first store allows 2 successive discounts of 23% and 28%. The other allows a discount of 35%. Which is a better offer?

3. One of the angles of a triangle is equal to the sum of the remaining two angles. If the ratio of these two angles is 5 : 4, find the angles of the triangle.

4. Evaluate without calculating the squares: $(205)^2 - (195)^2$

5. If $\frac{x+1}{x} = 11$, find the value of $\frac{x^2+1}{x^2}$.

6. Find the height of the triangle whose area is 30 cm² and base is 5 cm.

7. $\frac{a}{b} + \frac{c}{2b} =$ ....

8. Find the L.C.M of $(x^3 - 4x^2 + 4x)$ and $x(x^2 + 2x)$.

9. Solve $\frac{3y+5}{2-6y} = -\frac{5}{7}$.

10. 10% of 20 plus 20% of 10 = ...

11. The selling price (inclusive of VAT of 9%) of a washing machine is ₹13407. Find the marked price of the washing machine.

12. Mohan got an increase of 10% in his salary. If his salary after increase was ₹72,710, find the salary before increase.

13. Factors of $m^2 - 4mn + 4n^2$ are ....

14. Simplify : $\left[\frac{2}{3a^2 - b^2}\right]\left[\frac{2}{3a^2 + b^2}\right]$

15. Calculate compound interest on ₹12,000 @ 5% per annum for 2 years compounded annually.

Solutions

1	
2	
3	
4	
5	
6	
7	
8	
9	
10	
11	
12	
13	
14	
15	

Score

Exercise 20

1 Evaluate the expression:
$$\frac{(-2)^5 6^3}{(-2)^7(-3)^2}$$

2 $3x^2 - 3x(x - 1) - x(3 - x)$
$=$ ....

3 Find x: $\frac{(3x+1)}{8} + \frac{(2x-3)}{14} = \frac{(x+3)}{16} + \frac{(3x-1)}{7}$.

4 $\frac{2}{3}$ of a number when multiplied by $\frac{3}{4}$ of the same number makes 338. Find the number.

5 Factorise : $23xy - 46x + 54y - 108$.

6 Which of the following perfect square numbers is the square of an odd number?
289, 400, 900, 1600.

7

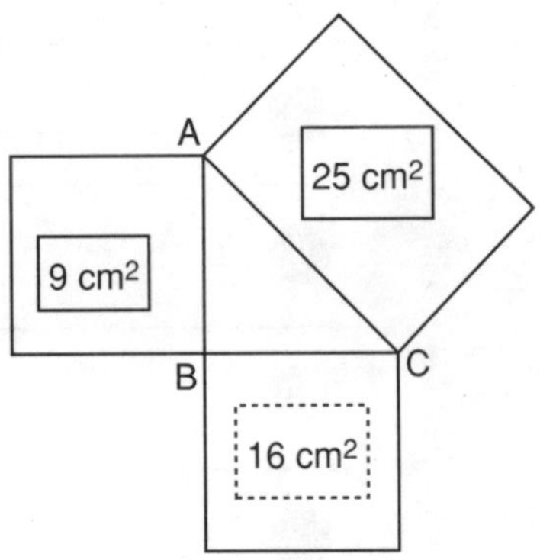

As shown in the figure above, the areas of the 3 squares are given. Find the perimeter of the ΔABC.

8 $153 = 1^3 + 5^3 + 3^3$
$370 = 3^3 + 7^3 + 0^3$.
Write any one more in this pattern. They are a part of Narticcissistic Numbers.

9 What is the value of
$$\left(1+\frac{1}{2}\right)\left(1+\frac{1}{3}\right)\left(1+\frac{1}{4}\right)\left(1+\frac{1}{5}\right).$$

10 Write p^2-$17p$-38 as the product of its factors.

11 Each edge of a cube is increased by 50%. The per cent increase in surface area of the cube will be ....

12 A number is divisible by 3 if ....

13 Find the compound interest on ₹12,000 for 3 years at 10% p.a. compounded annually.

14 At what rate of interest ₹400 would amount to ₹484 when compounded annually for 2 years?

15 Naman purchased an old bike for ₹20,000. If the cost of bike depreciates at the rate of 5% p.a. then find the cost of the bike after 2 years.

Solutions

1

2

3

4

5

6

7

8

9

10

11

12

13

14

15

Score

Exercise 21

1. If two quantities depend on each other in such a way that the change in one results in a corresponding change in the other, then the two quantities are said to be in ....

2. If the total cost of two tickets is ₹2400, find the cost of 8 tickets.

3. If x men can do a job in 'a' days, then '$x + y$' men can do the job in .... days.

4. If A and B can do a piece of work in p and q days respectively, then working together they can finish the work in .... days.

5. $y \propto x$ and constant of variation is 10. Find y when $x = 3$ and find x when $y = 25$.

6. 3 workers can paint a building in 12 days. If the work is to be finished in 4 days, find the number of extra workers required.

7. If $\frac{4}{7}$ of the tank can be filled in 2 minutes, how many minutes will it take to fill the tank?

8. A stationery seller pays ₹780 to buy 3380 pens. A month later he needs to replenish his stock and buy more pens. If the bill comes to ₹390, how many pens has he bought?

9. If 15 women can do a piece of work in 60 days, in how many days will 36 women finish it?

10. If the wages of 15 workers for 6 days is ₹9450, find the wages of 19 workers for 5 days.

11. A fort had provisions for 300 men for 90 days. After 20 days, 50 men left the fort. How long would the food last at the same rate?

12. If the cost of 17 metres of cloth is ₹340, then how much cloth can be bought for ₹840?

13. 14 pumps of equal capacity can fill a tank in 6 days. If the tank has to be filled in 4 days, find the number of extra pumps needed.

14. If 12 carpenters can make 480 chairs in 24 days, how many carpenters can make 1000 chairs in 24 days?

15. If 9 examiners can examine 135 answer books in 2 days then how many examiners are required to examine 540 answer books in 2 days?

Solutions

1.
2.
3.
4.
5.
6.
7.
8.
9.
10.
11.
12.
13.
14.
15.

Score

Exercise 22

1. Two persons are running from the same place at the speed of 9km/h and 6km/h respectively. Find the distance between them after 12 minutes, if they are moving in the opposite direction.

2. Avani covers a street 600 m long in 6 minutes. Her speed in kilometres/hour is ....

3. A speed of 9 m/s is the same as .... km/h.

4. Two trains of length 170m and 160m respectively are running at the speed of 50km/h and 40km/h, on the parallel tracks, in the opposite direction. In what time will they cross each other?

5. A train 140m long is running at the speed of 90km/h. In what time will it pass a man who is running at the speed of 9km/h, in the same direction?

6. Sunita and Raj take $5\frac{1}{3}$ hours to do a job. Sunita alone takes 16 hours to do the same job. How long would it take for Raj to do the same job alone?

7. A pipe can fill a tank in x hours and another can empty it in y hours. If $y > x$, the net quantity of water filled by both the pipes in one hour = ...

8. A pipe can fill a tank in x hours and another can empty it in y hours. If $y > x$, the time taken to fill the tank by both the pipes is ....hours.

9. A swimming pool is being drained through a drain at the bottom of the pool and filled by the hose at the top. If the hose can fill the pool in 21 hours and the drain can empty the pool in 24 hours, how long will it take to fill up the pool if the drain is left open?

10. Pipe 1 takes 5 days to drain a pool and pipe 2 takes 7 days to drain the pool. How long will it take for the two pipes to drain the pool together?

11. Rohit can dig a hole in 12 hrs. Ritu can do it in 8 hours and Sanjeev can do it in 6 hrs. How long will it take to dig the hole if they work together?

12. A can do a piece of work in 14 days and B can do it in 21 days. They began together and worked at it for 7 days. Then A was not well and B had to complete the work. In how many days was the work completed?

Solutions

Solutions
1
2
3
4
5
6
7
8
9
10
11
12

Score

Exercise 23

1. Every solid has three views: top view, ... view and .... view.

2. A brick is in the form of a ....

Name the types of polyhedrons in the following figures in Q 3 to 6.

3. 

....

4. 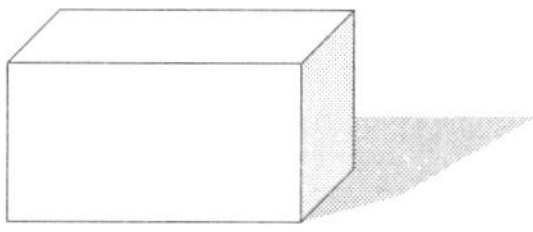

5. 

....

6. 

7. Identify the solid that can be made out of this net:

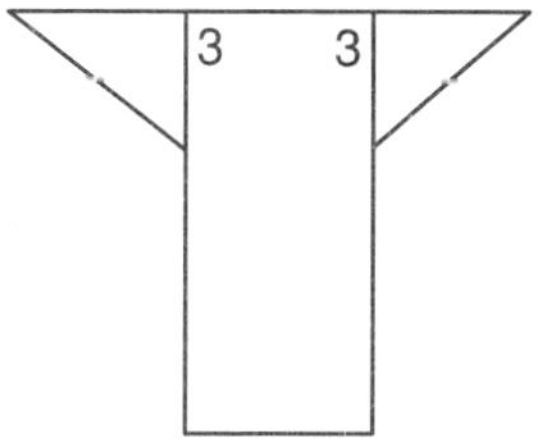

8. Identify the 3-D shape that can be made out of this net.

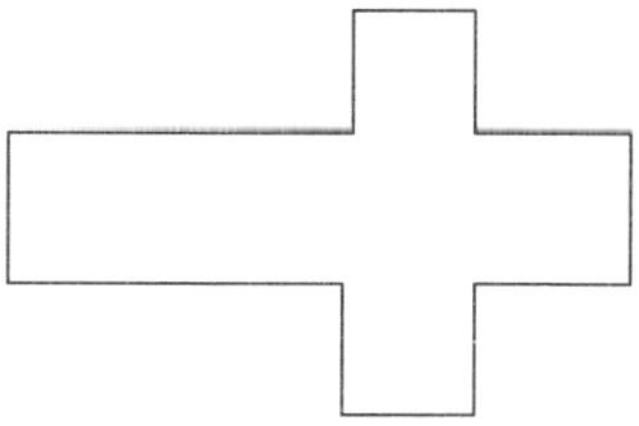

9. Platonic solids are regular convex polyhedrons in which all edges are of equal ...., all angles are of equal .... and all faces are ....

10. Name any platonic solid.

11. .... is also called a triangular pyramid. Its faces are congruent equilateral triangle.

12. To get more accurate representations of 3D objects in 2D, we use .... drawings.

13. Pyramids and prisms are named after their ....

14. Write the Euler's Formula.

15. Using a Euler's Formula, find the missing numbers.

Faces	–		5		6	8	–	
Vertices		12	–	–		6		6
Edges	30		8	12		–	9	

Solutions

1.
2.
3.
4.
5.
6.
7.
8.
9.
10.
11.
12.
13.
14.
15.

Score

Exercise 24

1. How many vertices, faces and edges does a rectangular pyramid have?

2. Sneha completes a work in 12 days and Vishal does the same work in 8 days. If they work together, in how many days can they complete the work?

3. Draw the front view of this figure.

4. On a scale of map, 1 cm represents an actual distance of 1,00,00,000 cm. If the distance between two cities is 350km, find the distance between the two cities on the map.

5. Which of the following is not indirect proportion:
   a. Less daily working hours, more men required
   b. Less days to finish the work; more men required
   c. more length of wall to be built; more men required

6. Two weavers A and B together weave a basket in 2 days. Alone, weaver A weaves the basket in 6 days. In how many days will B weave the basket alone.

7. On a scale of map, 0.8 cm represents 8.8 km. If the distance between two points on the map is 12 cm, the actual distance between these two points is .... km.

8. In a school, 9 periods of 40 minutes each are reserved in a week for Science. If the length of the period is reduced to 30 minutes, then how many periods in a week will be reserved for Science?

9. A and B can do a piece of work in 18 days. B and C in 24 days and A and C in 36 days. In what time can they do it, if they all work together?

10. A tank can be filled by one tap in 12 hours and by another in 6 hrs. How long will it take to fill the tank if both the taps are opened together?

11. For the given solid identify the top view, front view and side view.

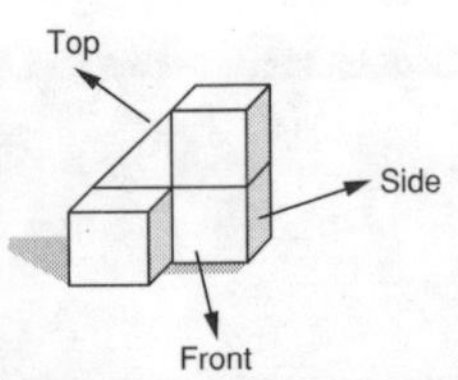

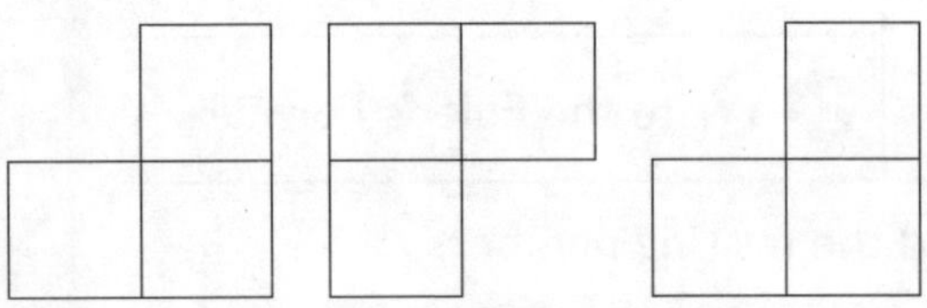

12. Identify the solid shape for which the net is given:

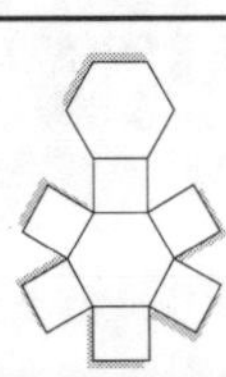

Solutions

1

2

3

4

5

6

7

8

9

10

11

12

Score

Exercise 25

1 If '*a*' and '*b*' are the lengths of the parallel sides of a trapezium and '*h*' is the perpendicular distance between them, then the area of the trapezium is given by ....

2 The area of a trapezium is 34 cm^2 and the length of one of its parallel sides is 10 cm and its height is 4 cm. Find the length of the other parallel side.

3 Find the area of a trapezium if its parallel sides are 6 cm and 8 cm long and the distance between them is 4 cm.

4 Find the height between the parallel sides of the trapezium, measuring 5.7 cm and 6.3 cm and the area being 24 cm^2.

5 If d_1 and d_2 be the diagonals of a rhombus whose side length measures 'a' units, then its perimeter is given by .... or ....

6 If the area of a rhombus be 24 cm^2 and one of its diagonal measure be 4 cm, find the length find the length of the other diagonal.

7 Find the area of a rhombus whose side length is 6 cm and the length of one of its diagonals is 8 cm.

8 If the diagonals of a rhombus are 10 cm and 24 cm,find the area and the perimeter of the rhombus.

9 The floor of a building consists of 2000 tiles which are rhombus shaped and each of their diagonals are 50 cm and 35 cm in length. Find the total area of the floor.

10 Find the area of the trapezium given below:

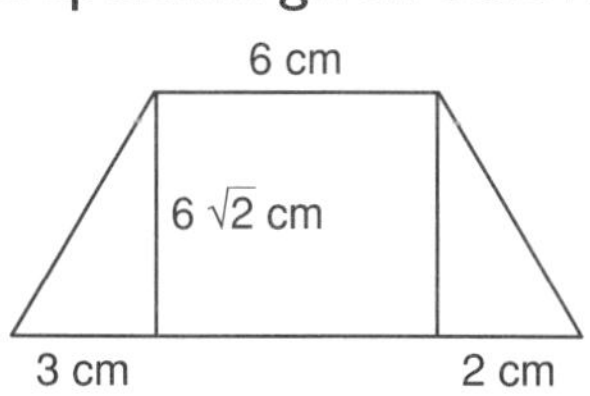

11 A rhombus has a perimeter of 100 m and a diagonal 30 m long. Find the area of the rhombus.

12 If the lengths of the bases of an isosceles trapezoid are as given below and its perimeter is 32 units, what is its area?

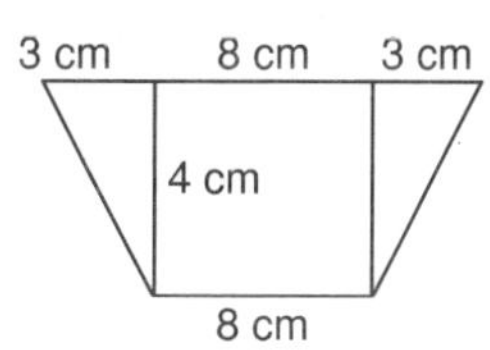

Solutions

1

2

3

4

5

6

7

8

9

10

11

12

Score

Exercise 26

1. Find the area of the pentagon ABCDE shown in the figure if DE II AC.

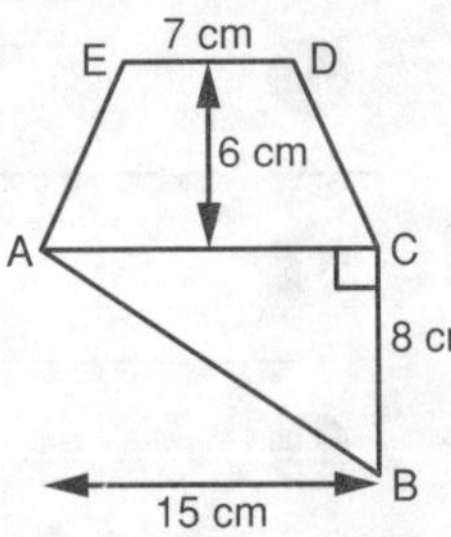

2. Find the area enclosed by the following figure as the sum of the areas of a rectangle and a trapezium.

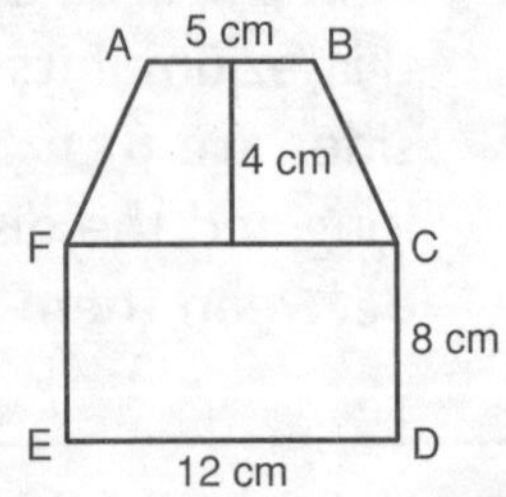

3. Two cubes each of 20cm edge are joined end to end. Find the surface area of the resulting cuboid obtained.

4. The diagonals of a rhombus are in the ratio 1 : 3 and its area is 54cm^2. The larger diagonal of the rhombus is .... cm.

5. Area of a general quadrilateral is given by .... where 'd' is one of its diagonals and 'h_1' & 'h_2' denote the corresponding heights.

6. The area of a rectangular plot is 27,000m^2 and the ratio of its sides is 6 : 5. Find the length and breadth of the plot.

7. Find the area of the quadrilateral whose one diagonal measures 15 cm and the lengths of the corresponding heights are 2.5 cm and 1.5 cm.

8. Find the area of a regular hexagon of side length 4 cm.

9. The dimensions of a rectangle are shown in the diagram. Find the area of the shaded region.

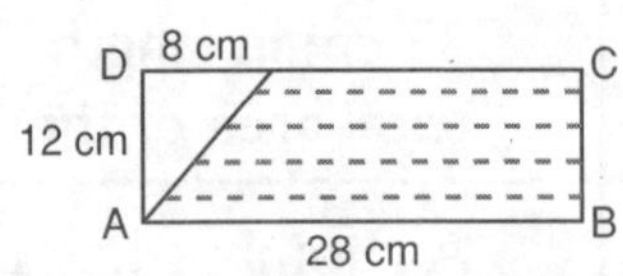

10. The diagonal of a quadrilateral is 30 m in length and the lengths of the perpendiculars to it from the opposite vertices are 6.8 cm and 9.6 cm. Find the area of the quadrilateral.

11. Find the height of the triangle whose base is 80 cm and the area is 0.08 m^2.

12. The area of a trapezium is 105 cm^2 and its height is 7 cm. If one of the parallel sides is longer than the other by 6 cm, find the two parallel sides.

Solutions

1

2

3

4

5

6

7

8

9

10

11

12

Score

Exercise 27

1. The lateral surface area in case of a cylinder is also called .... area.

2. Write the formula for the lateral surface area of a cube with length '*l*', breadth '*b*' and height '*h*'.

3. If '*r*' is the radius of the base and '*h*' is the height of the cylinder, then its total surface area is given by ....

4. Area of four walls of a room with length '*l*', breadth '*b*' and height '*h*' is given by ....

5. Find the total surface area of a chalk box whose height, length and breadth are 25 cm, 20 cm & 15 cm respectively.

6. A small indoor green house is made entirely of glass plates (including base) held together with a tape. How much tape is needed for all 12 edges?

7. In a marriage hall, there are 15 cylindrical pillars. The radius of each pillar is 18 cm and height is 3 m. Find the total cost of painting the curved surface area of all the pillars @ ₹10 per m^2

8. A five cubic cm cube is painted on all sides. If it sliced into 1 cc cube, how many 1 cc cubes will have exactly one of there sides painted?

9. Curved surface area of a right circular cylinder is 44π cm^2. If its height is 11 cm, find the radius of the base of the cylinder.

10. Two equal cubes with sides 6 cm are placed one above the other, forming a cuboid. Find the total surface area of the cuboid thus formed.

11. A rectangular piece of paper of width 20 cm and length 44 cm is rolled along its width to form a cylinder. What is the curved surface area of the cylinder so formed?

12. Find the cost of making a rectangular tank without a lid which is 1.8 m long, 1.2 m wide and 1.4 m deep @ ₹8 per dm^2.

13. The total surface area of the cuboid formed by joining 3 cubes each of edge 3 cm, side by side, is ....

14. Find the cost of painting 4 walls of a room, 10 m long, 5m broad and 6 m high @ ₹4 per m^2.

15. Find the surface area of a rectangular prism that is 8 m long, 6m wide and 2 m high.

Solutions

1.
2.
3.
4.
5.
6.
7.
8.
9.
10.
11.
12.
13.
14.
15.

Score

Exercise 28

1. What is the volume of the cuboid having $l = 8$ cm, $b = 4$ cm and $h = 5$ cm?

2. One face of the cube has an area of 25 cm^2. What is its volume?

3. The surface area of a cube is 96 cm^2. What is the length of one side? What is its volume ?

4. The cuboid has 3 different sized faces. The areas of two of the faces are 84 cm^2 and 56 cm^2. The volume of the cuboid is 672 cm^3. Find the length, breadth and height of the cuboid.

5. A cubical of wood was cut into 8 equal cubes of sides 4 cm. What is the volume of the block of wood?

6. A cuboid is 9 cm long, 5 cm broad and 4 cm high and a cube has an edge of 5 cm. Which one has greater volume?

7. A brick measures 15 cm in length, 8 cm in breadth and 5 cm in height. How many bricks will be used to make wall of length 15 m, breadth 10 m and height 8 m.

8. A iron piece 12 m × 4 m × 40 cm was melted into square pieces of side 4 cm each. How many pieces were made?

9. A cubic meter = ... cubic centimeter.

10. One litre = ... cubic cm.

11. Volume of a cylinder with base radius 'r' and vertical height 'h' is given by ....

12. Calculate the volume of a cylinder which is 5 m long and 40 cm wide (in cm^3)

13. The curved surface area of a right circular cylinder of height 14 cm, is 88 cm^2. Find the diameter of the base of the cylinder.

14. Find the height of a cylinder whose radius is 7 cm and total surface area is 968 cm^2 .

15. The radius and height of a cylinder are in the ratio 5 : 7 and its volume is 550 cm^3. Find its radius.

Solutions

1.

2.

3.

4.

5.

6.

7.

8.

9.

10.

11.

12.

13.

14.

15.

Score

Exercise 29

1. Area of a regular hexagon of sides x units = ...

2. If the sides of a square x are three times those of square y then the area of the square x would be .... times that of square 'Y'.

3. Find the area of the trapezium whose parallel sides are of length 12 cm and 10 cm and the distance between them is 6 cm.

4. The area of a trapezium is 512 cm^2. The lengths of the parallel sides are 12 and 20 cm. Find the distance between them.

5. For a rhombus with area 144 cm^2, one diagonal is twice as long as the other. The length of the diagonals are .... and ....

6. A rhombus has its diagonals 9 cm and 4 cm. What is its area?

7. The area of a rhombus is 36 cm^2 and its perpendicular is 24 cm. What is its height?

8. If the diagonals of a rectangle bisect each other at 90°, then it is a ....

9. The diagonal of a quadrilateral is 20 m in length and the perpendiculars to it from the opposite vertices are 8.5 m and 11 m. Find the area of the quadrilateral.

10. A cuboidal vessel is 10 cm long and 8 cm wide. How high must it be made to hold 480 cm^3 of liquid?

11. The dimensions of a cuboid are in the ratio 1:2:3 and its total surface area is 88 m^2. Find the dimensions.

12. A cuboid has total surface area of 40 m^2 and its lateral surface area is 26 m^2. Find the area of the base.

13. How many 5 cm cubes can be obtained(cut off) from a cube whose edge is 20 cm?

14. The diameter of the base of a right circular cylinder is 42 cm and its height is 10 cm. Find the CSA and TSA of this cylinder.

15. The circumference of the base of a cylinder is 88 cm and its height is 15 cm. Find the volume of the cylinder.

Solutions

1	
2	
3	
4	
5	
6	
7	
8	
9	
10	
11	
12	
13	
14	
15	

Score

Exercise 30

1. A photograph of a bacteria enlarged 50,000 times attains a length of 5 cm. What would be the enlarged length of the same bacteria if it is enlarged 20,000 times in the photograph?

2. Ritika has a road map with a scale of 1 cm representing 19 km. She drives 76 km. What would be the distance covered in map?

3. If one pipe can fill a cistern in 12 hours, how much time will it take for 4 such pipes to fill it up together?

4. Pipes A and B alone can fill a tank in 12 hours and 15 hours respectively. Pipe C can empty the tank in 20 hours. The total work done by the three pipes in one hour is ....

5. Find the area of regular hexagon of side 8cm.

6. If each side of cube is tripled, the volume of the cube becomes .... times.

7. If a 3D shape has 6 vertices, 4 faces and 9 edges. Is it a polyhedron?

8. If a pyramid has 4 faces, then it is called a ....

9. Name any two 3D shapes that are not polyhedrons.

10. The area of the base of a right circular cylinder is 154 cm^2 and its height is 15 cm. Find the volume of the cylinder.

11. The radii of two right circular cylinders are in the ratio 2:3 and their heights are in the ratio 5:4. Calculate the ratio of their curved surface areas.

12. Length of diagonals AC and BD of a rhombus are 6 cm and 8 cm respectively. Find the length of each side of the rhombus.

13. Find the area of the 4 walls of a room whose length is 10 m, breadth 8 m and height is 6 m.

14. Explain, by telling which two sides of this quadrilateral are parallel, so that it is a trapezium.

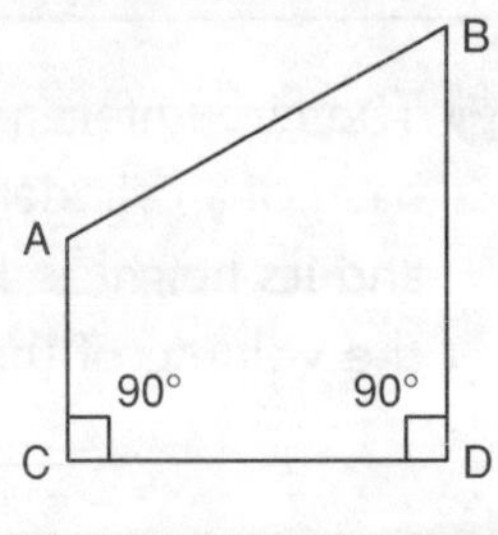

15. The dimensions of a cuboid are in the ratio 3:2:1. Its total surface area is 264 cm^2. Find the volume of this cuboid.

Solutions

1.
2.
3.
4.
5.
6.
7.
8.
9.
10.
11.
12.
13.
14.
15.

Score

Exercise 31

1. The given figure is a .... polygon.

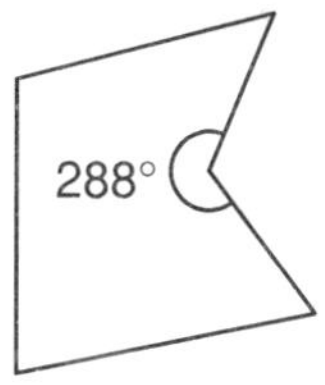

2. The given figure is a .... polygon.

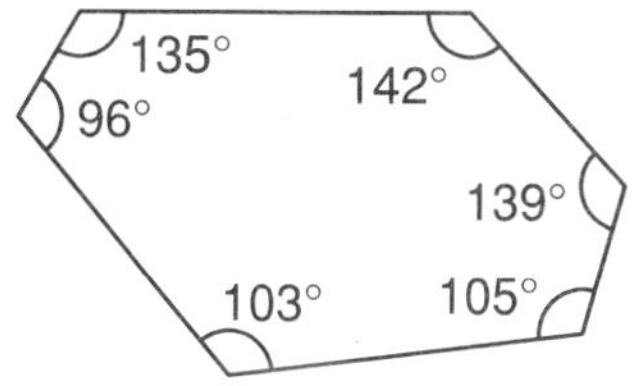

3. Sum of interior angles of a quadrilateral is ....

4. Find the sum of interior angles of a 9-sided polygon.

5. Find the number of sides of a polygon whose sum of interior angles is 1980°.

6. Is it possible to have a polygon whose sum of interior angles is 2049°?

7. Find the value of 'x' and the measure of each of the angle in the figure given below.

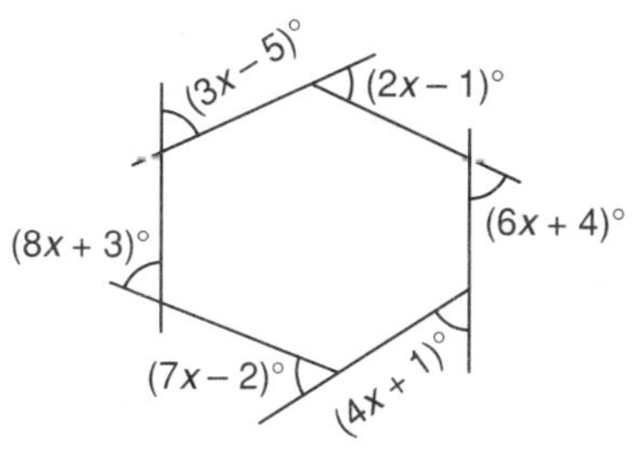

8. If each interior angle of a regular polygon is 120°, how many sides does this polygon have?

9. Find the number of sides of a regular polygon such that sum of its interior angles is 1260°.

10. Two angles of a quadrilateral are of measure 55° and the other 2 angles are equal in measure. What is the measure of each of these two angles?

11. The four angles of a quadrilateral are in the ratio of 7: 5: 9: 3. Find the measure of each angle.

12. The sum of interior angles of a polygon is 3 times the sum of its exterior angles. Determine the number of sides of the polygon.

13. Find the values of x, y and z in the following figure:

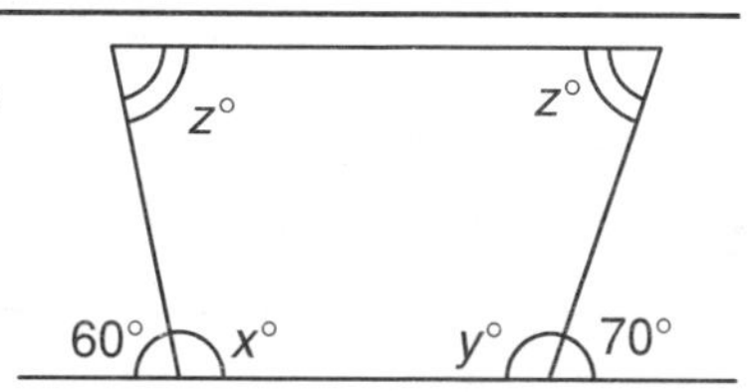

14. How many squares are there on a chess board?

Solutions

1.

2.

3.

4.

5.

6.

7.

8.

9.

10.

11.

12.

13.

14.

Score

Exercise 32

1. Two adjacent sides of a parallelogram have lengths 4 cm and 7 cm. Find the perimeter of the parallelogram.

2. In a llgm ∠ABCD, ∠C = 5y, ∠D = (2y + 30)°, find the value of *y*.

3. Find the length of the diagonal of a square whose side length is 5 cm.

4. PEST is a rectangle whose diagonals meet at a point O. If OT = 5*x* + 3 and OP = 3*x* + 7, find '*x*'.

5. Two adjacent angles of a llgm are in the ratio 1:5. Find all the angles of the ll gm.

6. Diagonal AC of a rhombus ABCD is equal to one of its sides BC. Find all the angles of the rhombus.

7. ABCD is a trapezium in which AB ll CD. If ∠D = 70°, ∠C = 40°, find the measure of the remaining angles.

8. The longer side of the llgm is 9 cm. If the shorter side is $\frac{2}{3}$ times of the longer side, then find the perimeter of the ll gm.

9. A trapezium in which non-parallel sides are of equal length is called an .... trapezium.

10. In a ll gm PQRS, the bisectors of ∠P and ∠Q meet at O. Find ∠POQ.

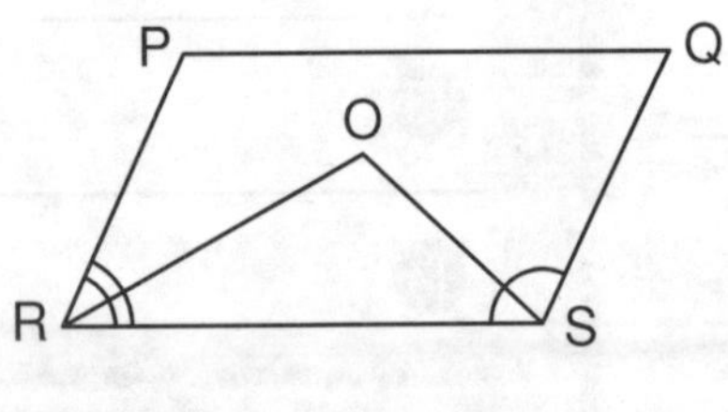

11. In a rhombus ABCD, AC is a diagonal. ∠ACB = 30°, find ∠BAC, ∠DCA and ∠ADC.

12. ABCD is a rhombus. If ∠ACB = 40°, find ∠ADB.

13. Identify the quadrilaterals whose diagonals meet at 90°.

14. A window frame has one diagonal longer than the other. Is the window frame a rectangle? Why or why not?

15. The angle between the altitudes of a ll gm, through the same vertex of an obtuse angle of the ll gm is 50°. Find the angles of the ll gm.

Solutions

1

2

3

4

5

6

7

8

9

10

11

12

13

14

15

Score

Exercise 33

1. How many elements are required to construct a unique convex quadrilateral?

2. To construct a concave quadrilateral .... independent elements are required.

3. Name the quadrilaterals whose diagonals bisect each other at 90°.

4. .... is a quadrilateral in which two pairs of adjacent sides are equal in length.

5. Is it possible to construct a quadrilateral TEAM where TE = 3 cm, EA= 4 cm, AM= 4.5 cm and TM = 2 cm and EM = 6 cm? Why/Why Not?

6. Name the quadrilaterals whose diagonals bisect each other.

7. Construct a llgm ABCD in which AB= 5.2 cm, BC = 4.7 cm and AC= 7.6 cm.

8. Is it possible to construct a quadrilateral FATE with FA= 5cm, FE = 6.5 cm, $\angle F = 105°$, $\angle A = 150°$ and $\angle E = 160°$? Why or why not?

9. Name two types of quadrilaterals which have diagonals of equal length.

10. Construct a rhombus whose side length is 4.8 cm and one diagonal is 5.6 cm.

11. Can you construct a square, if only its side length is given to you?

12. Name two quadrilaterals in which all sides are of equal length.

13. Construct a llgm, one of whose side length is 4.4 cm and whose diagonals are 5.6 cm and 7 cm Measure the other side.

14. Construct a trapezium ABCD in which AB = 7 cm, BC = 4.5 cm, CD = 4 cm and $\angle B = 60°$. Also AB II CD.

15. Construct a quadrilateral ZEST in which ZE = 6 cm, ES= 4 cm, $\angle Z = 60°$, $\angle E = 105°$ and $\angle S = 105°$.

Solutions

1	
2	
3	
4	
5	
6	
7	
8	
9	
10	
11	
12	
13	
14	
15	

Score

Exercise 34

1. A simple closed curve made up of entirely the line segments is called a ....

2. Name the polygon having 7 sides.

3. A .... is a line segment connecting two non consecutive vertices of a polygon.

4. What is the sum of the interior angles of a polygon with '*n*' sides?

5. What is the number of diagonals of an '*n*' sided polygon?

6. Find the values of *x*, *y*, *z* & *t*.

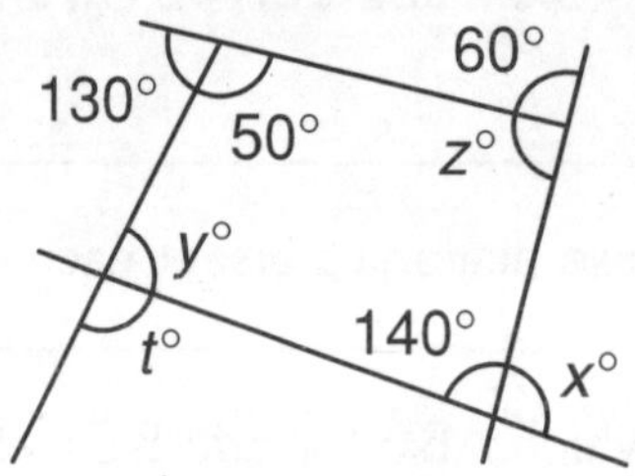

7. If two adjacent angles of a parallelogram are $(2x + 25)°$ and $(3x – 5)°$, then what is the value of *x*?

8. The diagonals do not necessarily bisect at right angles in a ....

9. Find the measure of each interior angle of a regular nonagon.

10. If in a parallelogram ABCD the diagonals AC and BD intersect at O, then OC = ...

11. The ratio of two adjacent sides of a parallelogram is 4 : 5. If its perimeter is 72 cm, find its adjacent sides.

12. A park in the town is made up in the form of a kite. Its perimeter is 90 mts. and one side is 10 more than the other. What are the lengths of its sides?

13. What do we require to construct a quadrilateral whose 3 sides are given?

14. What do we require to construct a quadrilateral whose 4 sides are given?

15. Can you construct a parallelogram with adjacent angles as 140° and 50°?

Solutions

1
2
3
4
5
6
7
8
9
10
11
12
13
14
15

Score

Exercise 35

1. A graphs is a .... representation of the collected data.

2. Which graph has a circular representation?

3. Name the mathematician who discovered the "Cartesian System" of plotting the points.

4. Name the point where the 2 coordinate axes meet.

5. The *x*-coordinate is also known as .... and *y*-coordinate is also known as ....

6. A line graph displays data that changes continuously over a ....

7. A line graph with unbroken line is called a ....

8. Give the formula for finding the angle of each sector representing an observation, in a pie chart.

9. The relation between .... variable and .... variable is shown through a linear graph.

10. A .... is a bar graph that shows data in intervals

11. A .... graph is used to represent two sets of data simultaneously.

12. What would be the perimeter of a square made up by joining the points A (0,0), B (4, 0), C (4,4), and D (0,4)

13. What would be the area of the right triangle made by joining the points *X* (0,0), *Y* (0,6) and *Z*(4,0).

14. In a pie chart, if the component values are expressed as percentage of the total value, then the central angle for a component = ...

15. The difference between highest and lowest values of observations in a data, is called .... of the data.

Solutions

1.
2.
3.
4.
5.
6.
7.
8.
9.
10.
11.
12.
13.
14.
15.

Score

Exercise 36

1. Name the study of collection, organization, presentation, analysis and interpretation of numerical data.

2. Collection of numerical facts related to a particular information is called ....

3. The number of times an observation occurs in a given data is called its ....

4. Organizing the raw data in a tabular form to know the frequency of each observation is known as making a ....

5. Name the first and the second number in a class interval.

6. What is the difference between the lower limit and the upper limit of a class interval called?

7. Name the term used to describe the average between the lower limit and upper limit of a class interval.

8. Data arranged in an order, whether ascending or descending is called an .... data.

9. What is the range of the data with following observation?
12, 17, 10, 45, 53, 28, 61, 44, 36, 28, 65

10. Bars in a bar graph are drawn .... or .... with equal spacing.

11. When the number of observations is large, the data is grouped into convenient ....

12. Find the frequency of 24 in the following data.
56, 29, 14, 24, 10, 7, 24, 7, 61, 29, 24, 56, 14, 10.

13. What is the class mark of 15–25?

14. A .... near the origin is used to depict that the graph is not beginning from the origin.

15. Tallies are usually marked in a group of .... for use of counting.

Solutions

1

2

3

4

5

6

7

8

9

10

11

12

13

14

15

Score

Exercise 37

1. Experimental Probability is based on .... where as theoretical probability is based on ....

2. Experimental Probability of an event 'E', P(E) = ...

3. Theoretical probability of an event 'E', P(E) = ...

4. Theory of probability has many applications in a branch of biology known as ....

5. When a die is thrown, list the outcomes of an event of getting a composite number.

6. One card is selected from a well shuffled deck of 52 playing cards. Find the probability of getting a black card.

7. Number 1 to 10 are written on ten separate slips and kept in a box. One slip is chosen from the box without looking into it. What is the probability of getting a 1-digit number?

8. If you spin a wheel with 3 green sectors, 1 blue sector and 1 red sector, what is the probability of getting a non-blue sector?

9. From a well shuffled deck of 52 playing cards one card is drawn. Find the probability of getting a face card.

10. Two die are thrown together. Find the probability of getting a sum 12.

11. What is the probability of getting the letter 'I' while choosing a letter from the word 'SIMILARITY'?

12. A dice is rolled. Find the probability of getting the number '7'.

13. Selecting a student from a class of 42 is a scientific or a random experiment?

14. If 2 die are thrown at a time, what is the probability of getting a sum '7'?

15. A coin is tossed 100 times and tail is obtained 52 times. Now, if a coin is tossed at random, what is the probability of getting a head?

Solutions

1.

2.

3.

4.

5.

6.

7.

8.

9.

10.

11.

12.

13.

14.

15.

Score

Exercise 38

1. The representation of numbers using bars of uniform width is called ....

2. A .... is a way of representing data using pictures or symbols.

3. Which graphical tool is used to compare or present more than one kind of information?

4. The number of times a particular observation occurs in the data is called its ....

5. The data represented by dividing a circle into sectors is known as ....

6. The x - coordinate is also known as .... and the y - coordinate is also known as ....

7. What is the class mark of the class interval 12.5–20.5?

8. What would be the central angle of the component whose frequency is 108 if the sum of all the frequencies is 540?

9. 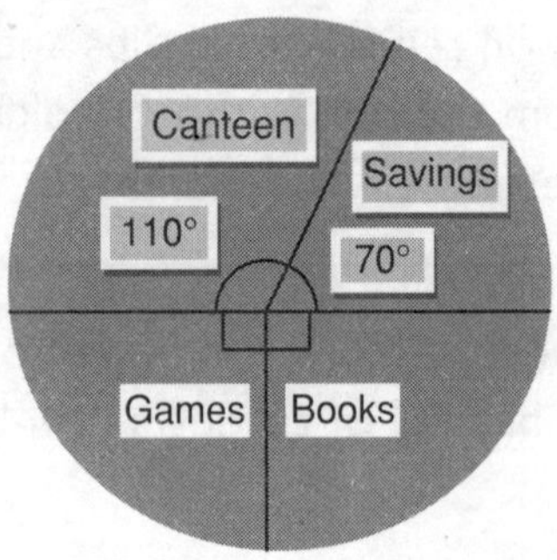

If Raj's total pocket money is ₹360, how much amount does he save?

10. Would the graph drawn by joining the following points be a linear graph?
(5,2) (5,4) (5,6) (5,8) (5,10) (5,12)

11. Find the probability of choosing a composite number between 50 and 60(both included).

12. What is the probability of choosing a consonant from the letters of the English alphabet?

13. If Sahil has 1 blue coloured, 1 red coloured and 1 white coloured T-shirt and he pairs it up with black or blue trouser, how many possible combinations can he make?

14. Number cards 50–100 are shuffled and placed upside down. What is the probability of getting a perfect square?

15. Two dice are thrown simultaneously. Find the probability of getting the same number on both the die.

Solutions

1.

2.

3.

4.

5.

6.

7.

8.

9.

10.

11.

12.

13.

14.

15.

Score

Exercise 39

1 In the following figure of rhombus PQRS, find the value of x, y and z.

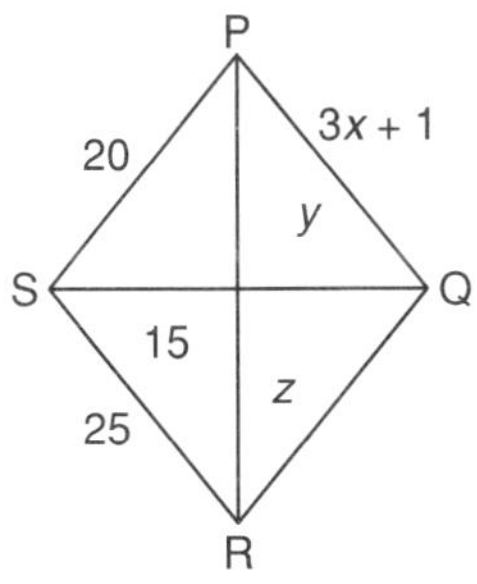

2 In the following figure of a parallelogram ABCD, find the value of x and y.

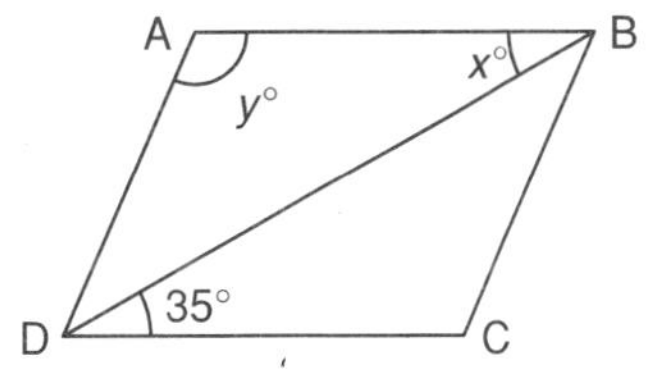

3 In the adjoining figure of parallelograms RICE and NEAT, find the value of x.

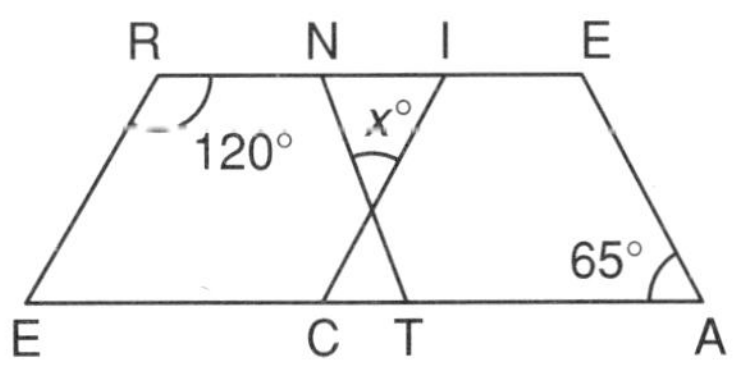

4 Name a regular polyhedron.

5 How many angle measures are required to construct a quadrilateral, whose 1 diagonal and 1 side are given.

6 Can you construct a quadrilateral having angle measures 105°, 95°, 150° and 15°? Why/why not?

7 A point whose y-coordinate is zero and x- coordinate is 5 will lie on ....

8 In Histogram, the height of the bars show the .... of the class interval.

9 A bag contains 5 blue cards, 2 orange cards and 4 red cards. A card is drawn from the bag without looking into it. What is the probability of getting a non- blue card?

10 Do the points A (6.5,0), B (6.5, 1.5), C (6.5, 2.5), D (6.5, 3.5), E (6.5, 4.5) form a linear graph?

11 At what points will the line joining (2, 3) and (3, 2) meet the X-axis and Y-axis?

12 What will be the length of the diagonal, if we construct a rectangle with adjacent sides measuring 6 cm and 8 cm?

13 What is the class size of the interval 0.5 – 0.10.5?

14 What is the probability that the sky is dark at 12:00 p.m.?

15 What is the probability that people would wear woolens in the month of June, in the Northern states of India?

Solutions

1

2

3

4

5

6

7

8

9

10

11

12

13

14

15

Score

Exercise 40

1. Draw the front view, top view and side view of a military tent.

2. 11 men can dig 6 m long trench in 1 day. How many men should be employed for digging 30 m long trench of the same type in 1day.

3. A train for 400 m long is running at the speed of 72 km per hour. How much time does it take to cross a telegraph post?

4. Maximum possible measure of the exterior angle in a regular polygon is ....

5. A pool is 20 m long, 15 m broad and 4 m deep. Find the cost of cementing its floor and its walls @ ₹12 per meter square.

6. The diameter of a garden roller is 1.4 m and it is 2 m long. How much area will it cover in 5 revolutions.

7. 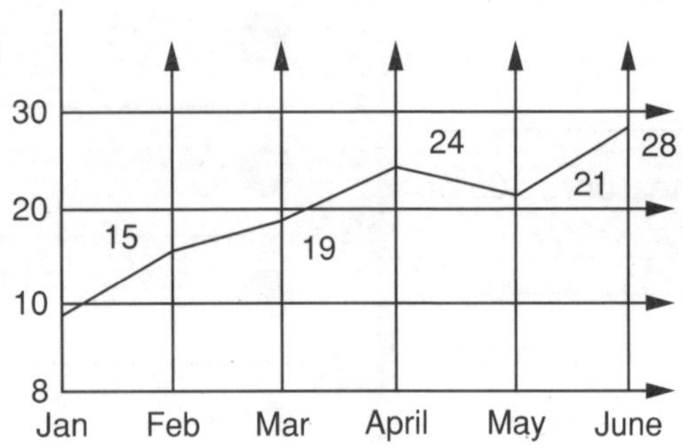

Given is the graph of the income (in thousands) of a family in 6 months. Find in which month the income was minimum.

8. Trapezium is quadrilateral with .... pair of parallel sides.

9. The .... is in a parallelogram are supplementary.

10. What is the maximum no of right angles in a right angled triangle?

11. How many diagonal does a triangle have?

12. Can u construct a quadrilateral ABCD in which AB = 5 cm, BC = 7.5 cm, angle A = 80°, angle B = 140° and Angle C = 145°?

13. In which quadrant does the point (–5, –1) lie?

14. In a lottery, there are 5 prizes and 20 blanks. What is the probability of selling a prize.

15. If a dice and a coin are thrown together, what is the probability of getting an even no. and a head?

Solutions

1.

2.

3.

4.

5.

6.

7.

8.

9.

10.

11.

12.

13.

14.

15.

Score

Solutions

	Exercise 1	Exercise 2	Exercise 3	Exercise 4	Exercise 5
1	Q, $-\frac{17}{23}$	Associative property of addition	729	$7 \times 1000 + 1 \times 10 + 8 \times 1$	3
2	$\frac{36}{-36}$	$\frac{8}{5}$	$q \times q \times q \times q \times q \times q$	11	$\frac{4}{3}$
3	$\frac{1}{4}$	$\frac{11}{9}$	$\frac{-9}{250}$	54	Yes as $\frac{-4}{17}, \frac{x-17}{4} = 1$
4	$\frac{-3}{7}$	$\frac{135}{-56}$	n	0 & 9	$74 \times 10 + 5$
5	(II) Pair	$\frac{1}{4}$	1	4, 9	$\frac{2401}{81}$
6	$\frac{0}{50}, \frac{0}{21}$ etc.	$\frac{-769}{933}$	$\frac{16}{9}$	$Q = 8$	Distributive property of multiplication over subtraction
7	$\frac{17}{70}$	$n = 3$	$\frac{4}{25}$	A = 5, B = 0, C = 1	-1
8	1. -1	$\frac{-1}{8}, \frac{1}{8}$	$(a)^{-6}$	Not Divisible	$1 \times 10^4 + 8 \times 10^3 + 9 \times 10^2 + 6 \times 10^1 + 4 \times 10^0 + 6 \times 10^{-1} + 3 \times 10^{-2}$
9	Zero	0 to -1	$\frac{-2}{3}$	(8)	Human hair is thicker than paper
10	$\frac{3}{8}$	There is no such rational no.	$\left[\frac{2}{3}, \frac{5}{7}\right]^5$	0, 2, 4, 6, 8	A = 1, B = 4, C = 5
11	0	$\frac{1}{9}$	$x = -2$	1340, 1430, 3140, 4130	$Q = 6$
12	$\frac{1}{Z}$	$-1, \frac{-2}{3}$	$\frac{-1}{18}$	15, 21, 28, 36	$\frac{1}{2}$
13	$\frac{ab}{b-c}$	$\frac{-17}{12}$	$\frac{xy}{x+y}$	$x = -3$	$\frac{25}{4}$
14	$\frac{1}{4}$kg.	$\frac{2}{13}$	$\frac{1}{5}$	$a - b + c$ should be divisible by 11	$(-y)$
15	$\frac{22}{13}$	$\frac{d}{c}$	$5^5 = 3125$	28	4.786346×10^3

	Exercise 6	Exercise 7	Exercise 8	Exercise 9	Exercise 10
1	$2n$	3	81	1158	$(p + 3)$yrs.
2	9	4104, 13832, 20683, 32832	209	Offer given by the first store	$(12 - t)$yrs, $(12 + s)$yrs
3	N	$\frac{\sqrt[3]{a}}{\sqrt[3]{b}}$	10	50°, 40°, 90°	$140a^4b^4c$
4	$6^2 = 36$	odd	276cm	4000	$-20a^2$
5	$1+3+5+7+9+11+13+15+17+19+21$	If $m < 0, m^2 > m^3$	No	119	$5x^2 - 7x - 9$
6	16, 63, 65	0, 1, 4, 5, 6 & 9	961	12 cm	$5x^2 - 2xy - 2y^2$
7	484	121m^2	Least no is 4	$\frac{2a+c}{2b}$	P^2
8	12	8:1	Least no is 2, squareroot is 50	$x^2(x+2)(x-2)(x-2)$	$-6pq^2s$
9	$144x^2$	No, if '+' is replaced by 'X'	27, 64, 125, – 8000	$y = 5$	$-10a^4 + 18a^2$
10	13	56	3cm^3, 3cm	4	$x^2 - 2x - 15$
11	$\frac{7}{10}$	1, 2, 3, 4 & 9	45 m	₹12300	$a^2b + 4a + 2b$
12	12	3	4	₹66100	$-\frac{9}{2} m^6n^6$
13	1.25	81	8 and 2	$(m - 2n)(m - 2n)$	$-3s^2u$
14	22.35	$120a^2$	5	$\frac{4}{9}a^4 - b^4$	10
15	None	$p = 8$	-175500	1230	24

Solutions

Q.	Exercise 11	Exercise 12	Exercise 13	Exercise 14	Exercise 15
1	$4a^2 - 6a - 28$	$4a^2b$	Linear	$X^3 - 9x + xy + 3y$	0.13
2	10096	False	$x = 4$	$25x^2 + 25y^2 + 48xy$	25%
3	$(x - y)(x - l)$	$x(x^2 + 2x - 1)$	$y = 2$	400	$x = 80, y = 80$
4	$(m^2 + 16)(m^2 - 16)$	$(2x - a)(x - a)$	$3x^2 + 22x + 7$	– 96mn	0.5%
5	$(q - 5)^2$	$(l - m)(l - m)$	$x = 5$	$x^2 + y^2 - z^2 + 2xy$	$\frac{1}{12}$
6	$(3xy - 5z)^2$	$(m + 2n)^2$	13	$z(2x - z)(2x^2 + z^2 - 2xz)$	$\text{S.P} = \frac{100 + \text{GAIN\%}}{100} \times \text{C.P}$
7	$2x - 3$	$(ax - by)(bx - ay)$	$x = 4$	$(y - 7)(y + 8)$	$\frac{n}{m + n} \times 100$
8	$x = 11200$	$\frac{4x}{4x + 2} = \frac{2x}{2x + 1}$	$x = 70°$	$(a + 1)(a^2x - ay - z)$	400%
9	$10 \times 5.74 = 57.4$	$m + 23$	$\frac{3}{5}$	$(ab + 3c)(ab - 3c)(a^2b^2 + 9c^2)$	S.P = ₹330
10	$3(y + 4)(y - 3)$	$x + 5$	$\frac{ma}{m} + ac$	$(2x + 3)(x + 1)$	M.P = ₹1000
11	$100^2 - 3^2$	$(a - 7)(a - 3) = a^2 - 10a + 21$	$x = 5$	$\frac{4}{7}$	15%
12	$q^8 - 1$	$(xy - 1)(y + 1)$	25, 45	Anil; 48yrs Ajith: 39yrs	Loss = (M.P – Discount) < C.P
13	$\frac{x^2}{25}$	$\left(\frac{1}{x-y-5z}\right)\left(\frac{1}{x-y+5z}\right)$	$x = 28$	L = 8units B = 2units	$100\,\frac{(y - x)}{y}$
14	7	$2 + x$	Cross multiplication	$y = -17$	M.P = ₹7000
15	20	$(x^2 + 1)(x^4 + x^3)$	$x = 14$	$x = -8$	S.T = ₹35 Bill amount = ₹735

Q.	Exercise 16	Exercise 17	Exercise 18	Exercise 19	Exercise 20
1	₹90	₹111360	₹775	1158	6
2	C.P = 500	R = 4.9%p.a.	Maths	Offer given by the first store	x^2
3	₹20620	P = ₹3200	$8\frac{1}{3}\%$	50°, 40°, 90°	$x = 5$
4	₹105	t = 8yrs	$\frac{146}{25}\%$	4000	26
5	₹900	₹561.6	2880	119	$23x + 54xy - 2$
6	8% Gain	₹1872.96	66500	12 cm	289
7	52 gms	t = 2yrs	₹6000	$\frac{2a + c}{2b}$	12 cm
8	Profit = 25%	₹64015	₹23329.97	$x^2(x + 2)(x - 2)(x - 2)$	$371 = 3^3 + 7^3 + 1^3$, $407 = 4^3 + 0^3 + 7^3$
9	$12\frac{1}{2}\%$	₹13400	Half Year	$y = 5$	3
10	₹1344	12yrs	5%	4	$(p + 2)(p - 19)$
11	44%	$\left[\frac{1 - r}{100}\right]^n$	4	₹12300	125%
12	₹176	$\left[P\left(\frac{1 + r}{400}\right)\right]^{4n}$	₹42000	₹66100	Sum of its digits is divisible by 3
13	Gain = $11\frac{2}{3}\%$	Quarterly		$\frac{4}{9a^4 - b^4}$	3972
14	Decrease of 1%	₹81000		$(m - 2n)(m - 2n)$	R = 10%
15	₹472.50	177366		1230	18050

Solutions

Exercise 21

1	Variation
2	1280
3	$\frac{xa}{x+y}$
4	$\frac{pq}{p+q}$
5	$y = \frac{5}{2}$ $y = 30$
6	6 workers
7	3.5 min
8	90
9	25 days
10	₹9975
11	84 days
12	42 metres
13	7
14	25
15	36

Exercise 22

1	3 km
2	6 km/h
3	32.4 km/h
4	13.2 sec
5	6.222… sec
6	8 hrs.
7	$\frac{(y-x)}{xy}$
8	$\frac{xy}{(y-x)}$
9	168 hrs.
10	$\frac{35}{12}$ days
11	2.666…hrs
12	4 days
13	30 days
14	10.5 days

Exercise 23

1	Side, Front
2	Non Polyhedron
3	Concave
4	Convex
5	concave
6	Triangular prism with right triangle as base
7	cuboid
8	Length, measure, congruent
9	Tetrahedron/ hexahedron/ Octahedron/ Icosahedrons/ Dodecahedron
10	Tetrahedron
11	isometric
12	Bases
13	F + V − E = 2
14	18
15	20, 5, 8, 12, 5

Exercise 24

1	E = 8, V = 5, F = 5
2	$4\frac{4}{5}$ days
4	3.5 cm
5	(c)
6	3 days
7	132 km
8	12
9	16days
10	4hours
11	Front view, Top view, Side view

Exercise 25

1	$\frac{1}{2}(a+b)h$
2	7 cm
3	28 cm^2
4	4 cm
5	$\frac{1}{2}(d_1 + d_2)$
6	D_2 = 12 cm, perimeter = 8
7	16 cm^2
8	175 m^2
9	Area = 120 cm^2 Perimeter = 52 cm
10	33 sq units
11	600 sq m
12	44 sq units

Exercise 26

1	126 cm^2
2	130 cm^2
3	4000 cm^2
4	18
5	$\frac{1}{2}d[h_1 + h_2]$
6	L = 5400 m, b = 4500 m
7	30 cm^2
8	24^2
9	288 cm^2
10	246 m^2
11	0.2 m
12	12 cm and 18 cm

Exercise 27

1	Curved surface
2	$4l^2$
3	$(2 + h)$
4	$2h(l + b)$
5	2350 cm^2
6	320 cm
7	₹509.10
8	54
9	2 cm
10	360 cm^2
11	880 cm^2
12	₹8448
13	126 cm^2
14	₹720
15	152 sq m

Exercise 28

1	160 cm^3
2	125 cm^3
3	64 cm^3
4	L = 12 cm, b = 8 cm, h = 7 cm
5	572 cm^3
6	Cuboid
7	20,00,000
8	3,00,000
9	1000000
10	1000
11	$\pi^2 rh$
12	628000 cm^3
13	R = 1 cm, d = 2 cm
14	15 cm
15	R = 5 cm

Exercise 29

1	$\frac{3}{2}x^2$ sq units
2	9
3	66 cm^2
4	32 cm
5	12 cm and 24 cm
6	18 cm^2
7	6 cm
8	Square
9	195 m^2
10	6 cm
11	2 m 4 m 6 m
12	7 m^2
13	64
14	CSA = 1320 cm^2, TSA = 4092 cm^2
15	9240 cm^3

Exercise 30

1	2 cm
2	4 cm
3	3 hours
4	$\frac{1}{10}$
5	96 cm^2
6	27
7	No
8	Triangular Pyramid
9	Cone, sphere
10	2310 cm^3
11	5:6
12	5 cm
13	216 m
14	AB‖CD
15	63888 cm^3

Solutions

Q.	Exercise 31	Exercise 32	Exercise 33	Exercise 34	Exercise 35
1	Concave	22 cm	5	Polygon	Visual
2	Irregular	$y = \frac{150}{7}$	6	Heptagon	Pie chart
3	360°	$\sqrt{50}$ cm	Square, rhombus, kite	Diagonal	Rene Descartes
4	1260°	$x = 2$	kite	$(n-2) \times 180°$	Origin
5	13	30°, 30°, 150°, 150°	No because of triangle inequality property	$\frac{n(n-3)}{2}$	Abscissa, ordinate
6	No	60°, 60°, 120°, 120°	parallelogram	$x = 40°$ $y = 50°$ $z = 120°$ $t = 130°$	Period of time
7	X = 12	∠A = 110° ∠B = 140°	No because of angle sum property of a triangle	X = 32	Linear graph
8	6	30 cm	Squares & rectangles	Parallelogram	$\frac{\text{Value of the component}}{\text{Total value}} \times 360°$
9	9	Isosceles	yes	140°	Dependent, independent
10	35°	∠POQ = 90°	Square, Rhombus	AO	Histogram
11	105°, 75°, 135°, 45°	30°, 30°, 120°		16 cm 20 cm	Double Bar graph
12	8	50°		17.5 m 27.5 m 17.5 m 27.5 m	16 units
13	X = 60°, y = 100°, z = 120°, w = 80°	Square, Rhombus		2 diagonals / 2 angles	12 sq units
14	X = 120°, y = 110°, z = 65°, z = 65°	No, diagonals of a rectangle are equal		1angle/ 1diagonal	$\frac{\text{Value in \%age of the component}}{100} \times 360°$
15	64	130°, 50°, 130°, 50°		No	range

Q.	Exercise 36	Exercise 37	Exercise 38	Exercise 39	Exercise 40
1	Statistics	Actual results, certain assumptions	Bar graph	$x = 8$ $y = 15$ $z = 20$	55 men
2	Data	No. of trials in which event E happened/Total no. of trial	Pictograph	$x = 35°$ $y = 110°$	20 second
3	Frequency	No. of outcomes favourable to event 'E'/Total no.of events	Double bar graph	$x = 55°$	120°
4	Frequency distribution table	Genetics	Frequency	Tetrahedron/ hexahedron/ Octahedron/ Icosahedrons/ Dodecahedron	₹6960
5	Lower limit, Upper Limit	4, 6	Pie chart	3	44 m^2
6	Class size	$\frac{26}{52} = \frac{1}{2}$	Abscissa, ordinate	Some of all angle = 365°	January
7	Class Mark	$\frac{9}{10}$	16.5	X-axis	Two
8	Arrayed	$\frac{4}{5}$	72°	Frequency	Adjacent Angle
9	55	$\frac{3}{13}$	₹70	$\frac{6}{11}$	One
10	Horizontally or vertically	$\frac{1}{36}$	Yes	Yes	Zero
11	Class intervals	$\frac{3}{10}$	$\frac{9}{11}$	(5,0) and (0,5)	No
12	3	O	$\frac{21}{26}$	10 cm	Third quadrant
13	20	Random Experiment	6	10	$\frac{1}{5}$
14	Kink	$\frac{1}{6}$	$\frac{2}{51}$	1	$\frac{1}{4}$
15	5	$\frac{48}{100}$	$\frac{1}{6}$	0	